The Question of Psychological Types

The Question of Psychological Types

The Correspondence of C. G. Jung and Hans Schmid-Guisan, 1915–1916

EDITED BY JOHN BEEBE AND ERNST FALZEDER

TRANSLATED BY ERNST FALZEDER
WITH THE COLLABORATION OF TONY WOOLFSON

PHILEMON SERIES

PUBLISHED WITH THE SUPPORT OF
THE PHILEMON FOUNDATION
THIS BOOK IS PART OF THE PHILEMON SERIES
OF THE PHILEMON FOUNDATION

PRINCETON UNIVERSITY PRESS
Princeton and Oxford

Published by Princeton University Press,
41 William Street, Princeton, New Jersey 08540
In the United Kingdom:
Princeton University Press,
6 Oxford Street,
Woodstock, Oxfordshire OX20 1TW

press.princeton.edu

Jacket design by Kathleen Lynch/Black Kat Design.
Jacket illustration: *Face in the Door* by Jean-François Martin. Courtesy of
Marlena Agency.

Library of Congress Cataloging-in-Publication Data

The question of psychological types : the correspondence of C. G. Jung
and Hans Schmid-Guisan, 1915–1916 / edited by John Beebe and Ernst
Falzeder; translated by Ernst Falzeder with the collaboration of Tony
Woolfson.
p. cm. — (Philemon series)
Includes bibliographical references and index.
ISBN 978-0-691-15561-6 (hardcover : alk. paper 1. Jung, C. G.
(Carl Gustav), 1875–1961—Correspondence. 2. Schmid-Guisan, Hans,
1881–1932—Correspondence. 3. Psychoanalysts—Europe—Correspondence. I. Beebe, John. II. Falzeder, Ernst.
BF109.J8Q84 2013
155.2′664—dc23

2012019327

British Library Cataloging-in-Publication Data is available

This book has been composed in Sabon LT Std

Printed on acid-free paper. ∞

Printed in the United States of America

10 9 8 7 6 5 4 3 2 1

Contents

Appendix

Acknowledgments

THE EDITORS WOULD LIKE TO THANK:

The Foundation of the Works of C. G. Jung; its director, Ulrich Hoerni; president, Daniel Niehus; and board members Christine Benz, Eric Baumann, and Felix Walder

The Philemon Foundation; its cofounder and general editor, Sonu Shamdasani; editor, Tony Woolfson; board members Nancy Furlotti, Judith Harris, Eugene Taylor, Caterina Vezzoli, and Beverley Zabriskie

Jung's daughter Helene Hoerni-Jung and Schmid's grandson Florian Boller, who graciously consented to informal interviews

Hans Konrad Iselin, whose German edition of these letters was frequently consulted

Princeton University Press, especially Fred Appel, Sarah David, Brian MacDonald, and Terri O'Prey

Readers Geoffrey Cocks and Adam Frey for advice and technical assistance

The Swiss Federal Institute of Technology (ETH), for access to the C. G. Jung Archive

Thanks also to the community of translators' forum at http://dict.leo.org/forum/.

Lieber Freund!

Wenn von zwei entgegengesetzten Typen die Typenfrage diskutiert wird, so besteht der grösste Teil der Diskussion im Vorbeireden und im Vorbeiverstehen. Die Sprache enthüllt hier ihre unglaubliche Unfähigkeit jene Schattierungen wiederzugeben, die zum Verständnis unerlässlich sind. So kann jedes Sprachzeichen Sinn und Gegensinn bezeichnen, sobald es psychologische Auffassungen decken soll. Wenn Du vom Extr. sprichst mit dem Gefühl der „identité mystique", so gelten natürlich viele Dinge, die ich vom Extr. sagte, ganz und garnicht. Ich sprach wirklich nur vom „ideal eingestellten" Extr., wobei ich es mit „ideal" nicht „ideal" meine, wie es z. B. in der Verbindung von „ideale Bestrebungen", ideale Überzeugungen" etc. gemeint ist, sondern „ideal" im Sinne von „seinem Princip entsprechend." Der Ausdruck „ideal" bedeutet in diesem Fall auch, dass der Idealtypus ein gedachter oder abstrahierter Typus ist, der in Wirklichkeit nicht vorkommt, indem der wirkliche Mensch natürlich auch den andern Mechanismus enthält, vermöge dessen er die Allzuschärfe des „Idealen" abzustumpfen weiss. Wo „ideale" der Fall ist, da ist's krankhafte [illegible]. Darum hast Du vollständig recht, wenn Du annimmst, dass ich hauptsächlich von „rohen" oder „krankhaften" Persönlichkeiten rede. Dort sind die „ideal Eingestellten" zu finden. Das Wort „ideal" ist eine [illegible] unbeabsichtigter Art. Im Gegensatz zu diesen Fällen sprichst Du vom compensierten Falle. Dort liegt die Sache natürlich anders. Du sprichst aber dann in der Hauptsache doch vom Falle „wie er sein soll" und nicht „wie er ist". Ich ging aber von der Annahme aus, wir sprächen von den „Typen" und nicht von den „Compensierten", an denen eben das Typenproblem m. E. schlechter zu erkennen ist, als am reinen Falle. Da Du nun einmal die Discussion auf den compensierten Fall verschoben hast, so will ich mich diesem andersgearteten Unternehmen anpassen.

Auf dieser Basis gilt natürlich mein Urteil über das Libido am Object nicht mehr, denn vermöge der Compensation erhält der Extr. ebenfalls ein Gefühl

First page of 7 J, 4 September 1915

Basel 17/18. XII. 15.

Lieber Freund.

Deine Reaktion auf meinen ehrlichen Brief hat mich nicht erstaunt. Da Du sie trotz meiner Fussnote nach Solothurn schicktest, kam sie erst heute Abend an. Ich habe sie nun durchgedacht und komme zum Schluss, dass sie ein Prachtstück mephistophelischer Weisheit ist. Der Schluss bewirkte ein wohltuendes Lachen, für das ich Dir von Herzen danke.

Schade ist, dass diese Wahrheiten für mich nichts neues sind. Ich habe einen ebenso scharfzüngigen Mephistopheles in mir, der mir dieselben Wahrheiten über Gott = Teufel, Eros = Giftmischer u.a.m. in noch plastischerer Weise schon seit langem gezeigt hat, besonders im schwarzen Buch.

First page of 12 S, 17/18 December 1915

Introduction

by John Beebe and Ernst Falzeder

JUNG'S *PSYCHOLOGICAL TYPES* appeared in 1921 to widespread acclaim and received many laudatory reviews.[1] In a two-page spread in the *New York Times Book Review*, Mark Isham concluded: "This volume is drastically serious, positive, didactic, classic, and yet more than stimulating. It is energizing, liberating and recreative. The author shows an amazingly sympathetic knowledge of the introvert of the thinking type, and hardly less for the other types.... Jung has revealed the inner kingdom of the soul marvelously well and has made the signal discovery of the value of phantasy. His book has a manifold reach and grasp, and many reviews with quite different subject matter could be written about it" (1923). *Psychological Types* has been one of Jung's most influential and enduring works, leaving an indelible mark on psychology, psychotherapy, personality testing, anthropology, popular culture, and even language. It was Jung's first major publication in nearly a decade since his 1911–12 book on *Transformations and Symbols of the Libido*. Yet there has been little study of either its genesis and elaboration from his first brief presentation on

[1] Sigmund Freud was not pleased, however: "A new production by Jung of enormous size [,] 700 pages thick, inscribed '*Psychologische Typen*[,]' the work of a snob and a mystic, no new idea in it. He clings to that escape he had detected in 1913, denying objective truth in psychology on account of the personal differences in the observer's constitution. No great harm to be expected from this quarter" (Freud & Jones, 1993, p. 424). Similar is Rank's report of Freud's view in a circular letter to the committee: "[The book] contains nothing new at all, and again deals with the way out he believes to have found, namely, that an objective truth is impossible in psychology, with regard to individual differences in the researchers. Such a result would have to be proven at first, however, since one could, with the same justification, also doubt the results of all other sciences" (Wittenberger & Tögel, 2001, p. 174).

the topic in 1913 or how his work on typology intersected with the self-experimentation he termed his "confrontation with the unconscious," critical details of which have recently emerged with the publication of *Liber Novus*, his so-called *Red Book* (2009). A vital piece of the puzzle lies in the present correspondence.

Its very first sentence, written by Jung on 4 June 1915, reads: "As you know from our previous talks, for the past few years I have occupied myself with the question of psychological types, a problem as difficult as it is interesting." Jung's occupation with this topic has indeed a long prehistory. As he went on saying in his letter to Schmid: "What originally led me to that problem were not intellectual presuppositions, but actual difficulties in my daily analytical work with my patients, as well as experiences I have had in my personal relations with other people." Five years later, he stated in *Psychological Types*: "This book is the fruit of nearly twenty years' work in the domain of practical psychology. It grew gradually in my thoughts, taking shape from the countless impressions and experiences of a psychiatrist in the treatment of nervous illnesses, from intercourse with men and women of all social levels, from my personal dealings with friend and foe alike, and, finally, from a critique of my own psychological peculiarity" (1921, p. xi).

Repeatedly, Jung also mentioned another crucial motive for his interest in the type problem, for instance in his 1943 edition of *On the Psychology of the Unconscious*, where he wrote of the "dilemma" into which he was put by the difference between Freud's and Adler's theories, the former placing "the emphasis ... wholly upon objects," the latter placing the emphasis "on a subject, who, no matter what the object, seeks his own security and supremacy" (1943, § 59): "The spectacle of this dilemma made me ponder the question: are there at least two different human types, one of them more interested in the object, the other more interested in himself?" (ibid., § 61). Similarly, in his 1959 *Face to Face* interview with John Freeman, he stated that the starting point for his work on psychological types was less the result of some particular clinical experience than it was for "a very personal reason, namely to do justice to the psychology of Freud, and also to that of Adler, and to find my own bearings. That helped me to understand why Freud developed such a theory. Or why Adler developed his theory with his power principle" (in McGuire & Hull, 1977, p. 435). Barbara Hannah confirmed that "Jung often said that he wrote the book in order to *understand* the dissensions in Freud's circle" (1976, p. 133); this is in concordance with E. A. Bennet, who wrote that Jung's study of the Freud-Adler conflict was "the starting point of Jung's work on typology" (1961, p. 57).

Without doubt, what he described to Schmid as his "experiences ... in [his] personal relations with other people," or the "critique of [his] own psychological peculiarity" (1921, p. xi), also played a role. Hannah found that since "Jung's most convincing characteristic was never to ask anything of other people that he had not first asked of himself," "we may be certain that his own shortcomings were one of, if not the main, reason for the volume on typology" (1976, p. 133).[2]

Hans Schmid was not only a personal friend and travel companion but also a pupil and former analysand. In him, Jung found a counterpart to his own "type," with whom he could enter into a discussion and confrontation, testing out, so to speak, his developing thoughts on the type question on both a personal and a theoretical level. As he went on writing in the preface to *Psychological Types*, in the book he had "omitted much that I have collected in the course of the years. A valuable document that was of very great help to me has also had to be sacrificed. This is a bulky correspondence which I exchanged with my friend Hans Schmid, of Basel, on the question of types. I owe a great deal of clarification to this interchange of ideas and much of it, though of course in

[2] Ellenberger linked the development of this concept with what he called Jung's "creative illness" after the break with Freud (1970, p. 672). Without entering into a discussion of whether Jung did suffer such an "illness," it seems safe to assume that his experiences during the period of his "confrontation with the unconscious" added to his understanding of the processes of introversion and extraversion.

altered and greatly revised form, has gone into my book" (ibid., pp. xi–xii).

Editorial History and Editorial Guidelines

The present correspondence was initially slotted for publication in Jung's *Collected Works*, and a draft translation was prepared to this end. On 1 October 1966, Richard Hull, the principle translator of Jung's works, wrote to coeditor Michael Fordham concerning the location of the Jung-Schmid letters in the *Collected Works*. He stated that coeditor Gerhard Adler wanted them to be published there, as he considered them too technical for the edition of Jung's letters that he was preparing (cf. Jung 1972a,b; 1973a,b; 1974). On the question as to whether they should appear as an appendix to Jung's *Psychological Types* or in the projected miscellaneous volume, Hull wrote that he had "painful doubts" over the first option:

> Certainly I would be hard put to it to say what Jung's views really were (in the letters) about differentiating the inferior function; he seems to be shifting his ground all the time, he comes out of it none too well in the personal sense, and the correspondence ends on a despairing, almost defeatist, note. It thus offers an ironic commentary on one of the main theses of the book: the desirability and possibility of differentiating the inferior function in the interests of interpersonal communication. On the other hand, it is a perfect illustration of the other main thesis: the existence of opposed psychological types who constantly misunderstand one another. What to do in this dilemma? I remember your saying in January that you found the correspondence tedious and long-winded, and, taking into account also its ambivalent and highly subjective nature, I'm wondering whether it is quite "proper" to include it in what is generally considered to be Jung's classic.[3]

[3] Richard Hull to Michael Fordham, 1 October 1966 (Michael Fordham Papers, Contemporary Archives, Wellcome Library, London). The extracts

Fordham replied unequivocally, stating his opposition to publishing the letters at all: "I would be in favour of leaving out the Jung-Schmid correspondence altogether. I found it unreadable, and if Jung wrote that the correspondence 'belongs essentially to the preparation,' I am against its inclusion anywhere."[4] Plainly, Jung's *Collected Works* was not conceived of as a historical, scholarly edition. In response to Fordham's position, Gerhard Adler fought for the inclusion of the letters. He wrote to Fordham:

> You have so far always maintained the attitude that the future student of Jung's writing should be given the fullest possible opportunity to see Jung's mind at work. For this reason alone, not to talk of its intrinsic value, I would plead strongly for retaining the correspondence in the *Collected Works*.[5]

Fordham, however, found the correspondence "very dull and not particularly illuminating" and not at a "standard required for public exhibition." He suggested that they put the matter to Herbert Read (senior editor) to arbitrate.[6] Adler agreed to this proposition, and reiterated that he was in favor of the publication of the letters because "they show an early phase of Jung's thought and how his later definitions arose out of a lot of confusions and struggle."[7] In their joint letter to Read, Fordham added a statement that clarifies what he meant by saying that the letters were not fit for public exhibition: "[T]he letters show Jung in a rather unfavourable light and that his tendency to fall back on his authority when driven into a corner may be all right in a private discussion, but it becomes rather embarrassing when displayed in public."[8] Without reading the

---

quoted from this and the following letters in this section were kindly made available by Sonu Shamdasani.

[4] Fordham to Hull, 10 October 1966 (Fordham Papers). Fordham had an aversion to psychological typology, which had little place in his own work (Fordham, 1978, pp. 6–8).

[5] Adler to Fordham, 16 November 1966 (Fordham Papers).

[6] Fordham to Adler, 18 November 1966 (Fordham Papers).

[7] Adler to Fordham, 20 November 1966 (Fordham Papers).

[8] Adler and Fordham to Read, 5 December 1966 (Fordham Papers).

letters, Read sided with Fordham and vetoed their publication.[9] This was enough to decide the issue, and the correspondence was not included in the *Collected Works*.[10]

It was only in 1982 that the first publication of these letters appeared, edited by Hans Konrad Iselin in the original German. In 2004 the Philemon Foundation was established, with the goal of preparing Jung's unpublished works for publication and attempting to fulfill the original intention of the project of Jung's *Collected Works* as Gerhard Adler and Michael Fordham saw it—namely, that it be complete. With the formation of the foundation, the possibility of an edition of the Jung-Schmid letters could be raised. Although it has taken decades for the correspondence to appear in English since first mooted in the1960s, it can now appear in a historical edition with full annotations, which would not have been the case had it been included in the *Collected Works*.

The present edition was accomplished in several stages. First, a new transcription was made of the letters, based on photocopies of the originals, kindly put at our disposal by the Jung Archives at the ETH Zürich (letters 1–9; with thanks to Dr. Yvonne Voegeli) and by Schmid's grandson Florian Boller, through the mediation of Ulrich Hoerni of the Stiftung der Werke von C. G. Jung (letters 10–13). Iselin's transcription was, where necessary, silently corrected. Second, a translation into English was made. Third, editorial and text-critical notes were added. Our guiding line in the editorial notes was to give contemporary readers factual information about anything with which they might not be familiar, or which might facilitate reading and understanding: persons, literary and scientific works, quotations, cryptoquotations, allusions, and so on, while avoiding judgemental or speculative statements as far as possible. Text-critical notes were made in cases when corrections, insertions, and margin notes by the correspondents were of any possible significance. Words that the writers of the letters had underlined have been reproduced in italics.

[9] Read to Fordham and Adler, transcript of carbon copy sent to McGuire, "received Dec. 13, 1966" (Bollingen Archives, Library of Congress, Washington, DC). William McGuire was the executive editor of the *Collected Works*.

[10] Fordham to McGuire, 13 December 1966 (Bollingen Archives).

Some minor changes were made to facilitate readability and understanding. In order to avoid passages that run over several pages we have broken up particularly long paragraphs. Abbreviated expressions and words—notably "e.v.," "i.v.," "E.V.," and "I.V." for extraverted, introverted, extravert, and introvert—were usually spelled out. Some commonly used abbreviations, however, such as "ucs." for unconscious, have been left intact. Anything added to the original text appears in square brackets.

Hans Schmid-Guisan and His Encounter with Jung

(by Ernst Falzeder)

Hans Adolf Schmid was born on 2 March 1881 as the third of five children of the silk merchant Johannes Schmid and his wife Sophie Anna, née Ballié von Rixheim. He studied medicine at the University of Basel, where he passed the state exam in 1905. He first worked as an assistant at the surgical ward of the Basel polyclinic and at the pediatric hospital. He obtained his M.D. degree in February 1907, and shortly afterward married Marthe Guisan. For three years he had a practice as a country doctor in the canton of Aargau but left it in 1910 to train as a psychiatrist at the Asile de Cery near Lausanne.

It was there, at a psychiatric conference, that Jung and Schmid met for the first time in 1911, as Jung stated in his obituary (1932, § 1714; cf. Freud & Jung, 1974, p. 426). "Not long afterwards he came to Zurich," Jung continued, "in order to study analytical psychology with me. This collaborative effort gradually broadened into a friendly relationship, and the problems of psychological practice frequently brought us together in serious work or round a convivial table" (ibid.). In December 1912 Schmid joined the Zurich branch of the International Psychoanalytical Association and gave a talk on "The Hamlet Problem" at its International Congress in Munich in 1913.[11]

[11] The talk was not published.

His continued collaboration and friendship with Jung included many mutual visits. Iselin mentions that Schmid's wife, Marthe, served both psychiatrists as a test person to find out whether free association was more fruitful when lying on a couch or when sitting in a chair—with the result that Jungian analysts to this day mostly prefer the sitting position (1982, p. 26). He also reports, referring to a personal communication of Jung's son, Franz, that they often sailed on Lake Zurich together and camped on an island in the upper part of the lake. "It was then that a wish must have grown in them to build a refuge with simple means in natural surroundings" (ibid., p. 19). Schmid realized this by erecting a primitive cabin in the village of Prêles, and Jung, as is well known, with his tower in Bollingen.

In July 1913 Schmid moved back to Basel, where he settled into private psychiatric practice and was soon known as *Seelenschmid*—a smith (*Schmied*) of souls (*Seelen*). "His 'deep warmth, his open geniality, and his cheerful personality'—as he was characterized in an obituary … —were much appreciated by his patients, one of whom once said that there would be nobody who could listen better than Hans Schmid" (ibid., p. 18).

Jung himself characterized Schmid in a letter to Henry A. Murray as follows:

> Dr. Schmid-Guisan is a friend of mine and quite allright [*sic*] inasmuch as there is no particular demand for philosophical or scientific clarity.… He is a very decent and good man, rather original and profoundly extraverted, artistic and intuitive. I often send patients to him. (2 May 1925; Harvard Archives, Cambridge, Massachusetts)[12]

Schmid was not a prolific writer or an important theoretician, but he lectured regularly and wrote a few scientific papers, as well as some novelistic essays and poems. Shortly before his death appeared his novel, *Tag und Nacht* [*Day and Night*] (1931), to which Jung wrote a preface (1931).

[12] With thanks to Sonu Shamdasani.

In 1932 Schmid received a minor injury and was treated by a colleague, but he acquired blood sepsis and had to be hospitalized. He died on 21 April 1932, only fifty-one years old. Hans Schmid-Guisan was buried near his cabin lodge in Prêles.

On 25 April 1932, Jung published a short but moving obituary in the *Basler Nachrichten* (see the appendix). "The death of Dr. Schmid of Basel," as Emma Jung wrote to Jungian analyst Wolfgang M. Kranefeldt, had "touched" herself and her husband "deeply.... It seems to me that just then he stood before an important turning point, and it is very tragic that the turn could not be made under the terms of life. Perhaps he was too little aware of the critical moment, or had just reached his limit, so that a different orientation (2nd half of life; his attitude was much too youthful) was no longer possible."[13]

The Prehistory of Jung's Concept of Psychological Types

(by Ernst Falzeder)

Already in his study on "The associations of normal subjects," written together with Franz Riklin (1904/5), Jung had found that "some individuals tend to react with internal associations and others with external ones" (ibid., § 382). In other words, there is a "type in whose reactions subjective, often feeling-toned experiences are used," and there is another "type whose reactions show an objective, impersonal tone" (ibid., § 412).

In 1909 Jung first introduced the term *introversion* in one of his talks at Clark University, in which he discussed the case of his own daughter Agathli (1910, § 13).[14] There he defined

[13] Letter of 2 June 1932 (Zentralbibliothek Zürich). With thanks to Sonu Shamdasani.

[14] Jung himself confirmed this in *Transformations and Symbols of the Libido*, referring to "the term 'introversion' (which I have ... introduced in my article 'Psychic conflicts in a child')" (1911/12, p. 32). Freud adopted the term, which he called "felicitous" [*treffend*] (1912a, p. 102; trans. mod.), though he did qualify this in a footnote, which probably referred to Jung's concept of

it as a process, in which a part of the love that before had been directed to an object in the outer world was turned inward, "introverted," resulting in an increase of fantasy activity.

He again used the term in (the second part of) the original edition of *Transformations and Symbols of the Libido*, where he writes: "It is generally to be expected that the two basic mechanisms in psychoses, transference and introversion, are to a great extent also very expedient normal modes of reaction to complexes: transference as a means to flee from the complex into reality, introversion as a means to detach oneself, with the complex, from reality" (Jung, 1911/12, p. 182).[15] That by "transference" Jung meant what he later called "extraversion" is shown by how he changed this passage later on, and as it can now be found in the *Collected Works*. There it says: "As one would expect, the two fundamental mechanisms *of the psyche*, *extraversion* and introversion, are also to a large extent the normal and appropriate ways of reacting to complexes—*extraversion* as a means of escaping from the complex into reality, introversion as a means of detaching oneself from external reality through the complex" (CW 5, § 259; emphasis added).[16]

In an unpublished review of Adler's magnum opus, *The Neurotic Character* (1912),[17] Jung wrote that Adler's overall

---

"introversion psychosis or neurosis" (Jung, 1911/12, p. 32), "[e]ven though some of Jung's remarks give the impression that he regards this introversion as something which is characteristic of dementia praecox and does not come into account in the same way in other neuroses" (Freud, 1912a, p. 102; "dementia praecox" was the term for the syndrome that is now known under Bleuler's [1908, 1911] term "schizophrenia"). Jung replied in a letter to Freud: "So far as the concept of introversion is concerned, I consider it to be a universal phenomenon, though it has a special significance in Dem. praec." (Freud & Jung, 1974, p. 486). Freud used the term nineteen times in his own works, for the last time in 1920 in *Beyond the Pleasure Principle* (1920, p. 51; cf. Guttman et al., 1995).

[15] My translation from the original German edition.

[16] In a footnote of 1912, not kept in the 1952 and CW editions, Jung added: "Introversion = going into the mother, sinking into one's own inner world or libido source" (Jung, 1911/12, p. 332).

[17] Only "a handwritten manuscript of it exists, entitled 'On the theory of psychoanalysis: review of a few new works' " (Shamdasani, 2003, p. 56).

approach was finalistic, whereas Freud's was essentially causal, claiming "that the preference for the final or causal standpoint was temperamental, as James had ... shown apropos the 'tough-minded' and 'tender-minded' in philosophy.... [W]hat was at work in the Adler-Freud opposition was a clash of unconscious world views" (in Shamdasani, 2003, p. 57). The impact of James's distinction between rationalists (the "tender-minded") and empiricists (the "tough-minded"), as well as of his views on pragmatism and pluralism, upon Jung's work has also been shown by Shamdasani (ibid., pp. 58–61).

It is not entirely clear when Jung first used the term "extraversion." Iselin (1982, p. 137) writes that it was in his talk on 8 September 1913, at the Fourth International Psychoanalytical Congress in Munich, which seems unlikely, since in that talk, as originally delivered in German, Jung referred to introversion and extraversion as two concepts he had already introduced *before* ("Ich *habe* diese zwei ... Richtungen der Libido 'Extraversion' und 'Introversion' *genannt*"; Jung, 1913a, § 860; emphasis added).[18] In any case, there is no mentioning of extraversion in any published works[19] of Jung's before the Munich talk.

There, Jung defined the two types as follows: "We speak of extraversion when he [the individual] gives his whole interest to the outer world, to the object, and attributes an extraordinary importance and value to it. When, on the contrary, the objective world sinks into the shadow, as it were, or undergoes a devaluation, while the individual occupies the centre of his own interest and becomes in his own eyes the only person worthy of consideration, it is a case of introversion. I call *regressive extraversion* the phenomenon which Freud calls *transference*,[20] when

[18] Unfortunately, the first English translation of this paper, carried forward into the *Collected Works*, lost the past tense, and the text simply reads, "I propose to use the terms *extraversion* and *introversion* to describe these two opposite movements of libido" (CW 6, § 860).

[19] That is, in their original form, as opposed to the later, reworked versions as they now appear in the *Gesammelte Werke* and the *Collected Works* (see Bibliography *Note* about Jung's works).

[20] Further evidence that Jung originally equated transference with extraversion, at least in the latter's "regressive" mode.

the hysteric projects upon the object his own illusions and subjective valuations. In the same way, I call *regressive introversion* the opposite phenomenon which we find in schizophrenia, when these fantastic ideas refer to the subject himself" (Jung, 1913a, § 860).

Jung quoted seven authors who had made comparable distinctions before him. In addition to William James, who, according to Jung, had made "the best observations in this respect" (ibid., § 864), and his juxtaposition of the tender- and the tough-minded, he mentioned Wilhelm Ostwald (romanticists vs. classicists), Wilhelm Worringer (feeling-into vs. abstraction), Friedrich Schiller (naive vs. sentimental types), Friedrich Nietzsche (the Apollonian vs. the Dionysian), Franz Nikolaus Finck and his linguistic theory of "action verbs" vs. "sensation verbs," and Otto Gross (flattened and broadened consciousness vs. narrowed and deepened consciousness).

Among the authors he did *not* quote were William Stern, Alfred Binet, and Sándor Ferenczi.[21] In 1900 the German psy-

[21] John Kerr adds another author: "Quite possibly,... the important step that Jung took at the Munich congress [i.e., the introduction of his introversion/extraversion typology] had occurred to him while reading Freud's paper" (1993, p. 464), "Types of onset of neurosis" (Freud, 1912b). If true, this would be a quite sensational find—Jung being inspired to his probably most influential contribution to psychology by Freud himself. In fact, this is highly unlikely, indeed unthinkable. First, as has been shown above, Jung had already introduced the nucleus of this typology in *Transformations and Symbols of the Libido* (still using the term "transference" for extraversion), written before Freud's paper. Second, in his paper Freud merely described four types of precipitating causes of falling ill—and *not* psychological personality types—one of those causes being frustration [*Versagung*]. In that context he used Jung's already previously introduced concept of "introversion of the libido" to describe the effect of frustration, that is, the "risk of the libido becoming 'introverted,'" adding in a footnote: "To use a term introduced by C. G. Jung" (1912b, p. 232). There is no mentioning of anything similar to extraversion. What Freud did, however, was to draw attention to another cause, whose discovery "was in fact only possible ... through searching analytic investigations following on the Zurich school's theory of complexes" (ibid., p. 233): the inability to adapt to reality and to fulfill the demands of reality. Instead of being a source of inspiration, or even plagiarism, for Jung, then, Freud's paper in contrast freely borrowed from him and the "Zurich school" and openly acknowledged their contributions.

chologist William Stern had distinguished between objective judgement types, whose judgements were primarily determined by outer stimuli, and subjective judgement types, whose judgements were primarily determined by the state of the subject (cf. Shamdasani, 2003, p. 43). Alfred Binet (1903) had maintained that there were "two distinct typical forms of reaction" in associations to given words: "objectivism, the tendency to live in the outer world, and subjectivism, the tendency to enclose oneself in one's own consciousness" (Shamdasani, 2003, p. 42). Binet called these the types of (in French) "introspection" and "externospection." Oliver Brachfeld (1954) first drew attention to the similarities between Jung's typology and that of Binet, which Jung never quoted. Ellenberger, referring to Brachfeld, notes that Binet's book appeared when Jung was in Paris and that he might have read it and then forgotten it (1970, p. 703).

In 1909 Ferenczi published "Introjection and transference." There he stated that "[a]ll neurotics suffer from *flight from their complexes*" (p. 45). "[I]n order to escape from complexes that are unpleasant, and hence have become unconscious," the neurotic transfers, that is, he "is forced to meet the persons and things of the outer world with exaggerated interest" (p. 39). This "favours the emergence of day-dreams, first unconscious, later becoming conscious" (p. 43). In direct contrast to the paranoiac, who "projects on to the outer world the interest that has become a burden to him" and "expels from his ego the impulses that have become unpleasant" (p. 47), the neurotic (hysteric) "is constantly seeking for objects with whom he can identify himself, to whom he can transfer feelings" (p. 48). He takes "into the ego as large as possible a part of the outer world, making it the object of unconscious phantasies.... One might give this process, in contrast to projection, the name of *Introjection* [*sic*]" (p. 47). "The psychoneurotic suffers from a widening, the paranoic [*sic*] from a shrinking of his ego" (p. 48).

Although Ferenczi's description of the interplay of centrifugal versus centripetal movements of the libido is not completely congruent with Jung's concept of extraversion and introversion, there are some similarities, and it is worth noting that Jung fails to mention the work of his former student. But then, Jung's presentation has to be seen also before the background of Freud's break with Adler, and his own imminent break with Freud.

Coming back to Jung's Munich talk—which was given before this background—he stated not only that extraversion and introversion are characteristic of hysteria and dementia praecox respectively but that "there may also be normal human types who are distinguished by the predominance of one or other of the two mechanisms" (1913a, § 862). It was only in his concluding remarks, however, that he made, for the first time in public, a much more far-reaching claim: these two types would characterize not only *people* but also *theories*, and particularly theories in "analytical psychology" (ibid., § 880).[22] Thus, Freud's *theory* could be described as "extraverted," that is, reductionistic, pluralistic, sensational, materialistic, pessimistic, irreligious, deterministic, and causal, whereas Adler's was "introverted," intellectualistic, monistic, and finalistic. (Jung did not uphold this implied equation of an explanation by a *causa finalis* with introversion, and of one by a *causa efficiens* with extraversion, later on.) And not only would these types color the presentation of these men's theories, or influence the choice of topics they were dealing with, and from which perspective, but they would also lead, as Jung implied in his talk, and openly writes in the present correspondence, to "viewing the world in the light of *two truths*," and these two truths would be "two different, but *equally true*, perceptions of one and the same situation" (emphasis added). "The difficult task of the future," Jung ended his talk by saying, "will be to create a psychology that will do equal

[22]This in accordance with his view that "sciences ... are *symptoms* of man's soul" (1930/31, § 752; emphasis in the original). The term Jung used in the original German is *analytische Psychologie*, which was translated as "psychoanalysis" in the *Collected Works*. Jung seems to have first used the former term in 1912 ("New paths in psychology"; § 410) to designate the "new psychology" founded by Freud (synonymous with "depth psychology," which is Bleuler's term)—hence, clearly not in the sense in which he used it later on, namely, as one possible name for his own psychology.

justice to both types" (1913a, § 882, trans. mod.)—presumably his own, which he had already announced "seeks to maintain the balance between the two psychological opposites of extraversion and introversion" (ibid., § 872).

Quite a program to be announced at an official congress by the president of the International Psycho-Analytical Association, an association whose purpose was, as stated in the statutes, "the cultivation and promotion of the psychoanalytic science as inaugurated by Freud" (in Freud & Jung, 1974, p. 568). In fact, Jung declared—in Freud's presence, and in the absence of Adler, who had already left, or rather been forced to leave, the society in 1911—that Adler's theory was as valid as that of Freud, while both would still be wanting and one-sided, and all but announced that he was about to develop a third psychology, superior to Freud's and Adler's, and indeed to all other psychological theories.

In applying his typological concept not only to individuals but also to theories, Jung made a crucial extension of this concept, with considerable consequences. One consequence, which Jung clearly saw, was that (at least in psychology) this implied that there existed more than one truth: there were "*two truths*," "two different, but *equally true*, perceptions of one and the same situation." The point is that Jung then went on to develop still *another* "truth," namely, his own theory of psychological types, which would be able to explain why this was so. Implicitly, then, this latter "truth" was of a higher order than the other two "truths."[23] Implicitly, too, he thus claimed to have found, with his typology, an "Archimedean point," with the help of which he could move the world of psychology—even if he often explicitly stated that this was impossible.[24] Similarly, he writes in his exchange with Schmid:

[23] Jung found himself in a logical dilemma because he used two different concepts of "truth." The "two truths" he mentioned are actually just two different, if valid, *perceptions* of one and the same situation. In German the difference between the concepts would be that between "Wahr*nehmung*" (perception) and "Wahr*heit*" (truth).

[24] For example, in chronological order: "[W]e do not possess a physics of the soul, and are not even able to observe it and judge it from some Archime-

"The Archimedean point outside of psychology, with the help of which we would be able to unhinge psychology, is hardly likely to be found" (1 J).

This concept also highlights a crucial difference between Jung and Freud. For Freud, there was no doubt that—as in any other science—there was but *one* "truth" in psychology (and that he, Freud, had found it), and that there was a method to find it out, namely, psychoanalysis. When Jung objected that brilliant people (such as Freud, Adler, and himself), using the very same method, came to different, even contradictory conclusions, Freud would have countered: if this was so, then those who came to results different from those he had reached himself must have used the method incorrectly, or were, for personal reasons (resistances), unable to see the obvious. No, Jung would reply, even if Freud's and Adler's theories were correct to some extent, and in that sense "true," they would not tell the *whole* truth.

In December of the same year, Jung published his Munich talk in French,[25] under the title "Contribution à l'étude des types psychologiques," in *Archives de Psychologie* (Jung, 1913a).

---

dean point 'outside' ourselves, and can therefore know nothing objective about it since all knowledge of the psyche is itself psychic" (1911/12, § 344). "[P]sychology ... lacks the Archimedean point outside and hence the possibility of objective measurement" (1926, § 163). "[T]he mind cannot apprehend its own form of existence, owing to the lack of an Archimedean point outside" (1938[1937], § 18; cf. ibid., §§ 87, 377). "To inquire into the *substance* of what has been observed is possible in natural science only where there is an Archimedean point outside. For the psyche, no such outside standpoint exists" (1945/46, § 384). "[P]sychology ... lacks the immense advantage of an Archimedean point such as physics enjoy" (1946/47, § 421). "I do not imagine for a moment that I can stand above or beyond the psyche, so that it would be possible to judge it, as it were, from some transcendental Archimedean point 'outside' " (1951, § 254). Jung maintained, however, that a "spiritual goal that points beyond the purely natural man and his worldly existence is an absolute necessity for the health of the soul; it is the Archimedean point from which alone it is possible to lift the world off its hinges and to transform the natural state into a cultural one" (1926, § 159).

[25] Interestingly, he did not publish his presidential address in the organ of the International Psycho-Analytical Association, the *Jahrbuch*, of which he was still the managing editor.

In his review of this article, Ferenczi (1914)[26] criticized precisely Jung's extension of the concept to also encompass theories: "This classification doubtlessly offers some interesting perspectives. Questionable is only the last passage of the article, however, in which Jung wants to extend his ... classification also to psychology itself.... We believe that Jung ... let himself be carried away to an all too complicated and psychologizing explanation" (ibid., p. 65). The difference between Freud's and Adler's theories would not be that one was the product of an extraverted, "tough-minded" thinker, and the other of an introverted, "tender-minded" one, but simply that Freud developed a psychology of the unconscious, while Adler dealt with the psychology of consciousness (ibid., p. 66).

In 1914, in a supplement to the second edition of his monograph *The Content of the Psychoses,* Jung wrote: "The terms introversion and extraversion are dependent on my energic conception of psychic phenomena. I postulate a hypothetical fundamental striving which I call *libido*" (1914a, § 418; emphasis in the original). And he went on saying: "The introverted type directs his libido chiefly to his own personality: he finds the absolute value in himself. The extraverted type directs his libido outwards: he finds the absolute value in the object.... I ... would ... like to emphasize that *the type question is one of the most vital for our psychology and that any further advance will probably be along those lines....* In the realm of medical psychology, Freud is decidedly the champion of the extravert, Adler the champion of the introvert. The irreconcilable contradiction between the views of Freud and Adler... is easily explained by the existence of two diametrically opposed psychologies which view the same things under totally different aspects" (ibid., § 419; emphasis added).[27]

[26]This review has not yet been translated into English. Quotes are my translation from the original German.

[27]In a letter to Smith Ely Jelliffe of 5 March 1915, Jung confirmed that during that time he had been "especially working about the two types of psychology and about the synthesis of unconscious tendencies" (Burnham, 1983, pp. 196–97).

This was Jung's point of view at the time when his correspondence with Hans Schmid, conducted from 4 June 1915 to 6 January 1916, began.[28]

The Correspondence and the Correspondents

(by John Beebe)

Jung seems to have suggested the correspondence with Schmid as a kind of Platonic dialogue, a dialectical discourse. Schmid was someone who he had decided, on the basis of "previous talks," could instinctively[29] articulate the position of an extravert, while he, Jung, could as naturally argue that of an introvert. Their temperamental capacities created the basis for a conversation that would illustrate, as well as intellectually circumambulate, the problem of different kinds of truth based on psychological type. The men were friends, and Jung felt that Schmid would be willing on that basis too to take up "the question of psychological types" with him in an honest exchange in which each would be free to speak openly to the other. Jung, having thought longer and harder about the type problem, would naturally take the lead. Schmid confirms this at the beginning of his first reply to Jung (2 S), when he assures Jung: "As you have guessed, dealing further with the question of the psychological types has not given me any real

[28] At the time, Jung was also working on his so-called Black Books which formed the template for the *Liber Novus* or *Red Book* (Jung, 2009). As Shamdasani notes, the "*Black Books* run consecutively until July 21, 1914, and recommence on June 3, 1915. In the hiatus, Jung wrote the *Handwritten Draft*" (ibid., pp. 225–26). Shamdasani also points to the fact (personal communication) that the next entry in the Black Books is only on 14 September 1915, so it is clear that the bulk of Jung's discussions with Schmid took place during that pause, and that he then returned to the Black Books.

[29] In his obituary of Schmid, Jung wrote: "At that time we were especially interested in the question of the relativity of psychological judgments, or in other words, the influence of temperament on the formation of psychological concepts. As it turned out, he developed instinctively an attitude type which was the direct opposite of my own" (1932, § 1714).

headaches." He makes it clear, however, that he is not going to accept Jung's premise that the two types are *not* going to be able to understand each other.

Schmid's relative optimism reflects his belief in the possibilities of relationship. This value he upholds throughout the correspondence, even to the point of continuing to write to Jung after the latter, with a touch of exasperation, has announced that he has penned his "last" letter (9 J) in it. Schmid also is willing to argue his position on intellectual grounds: "I have never viewed the problem of the types as the existence of two truths, however, but I rather envisaged, from the genetic point of view, the existence of two poles between which psychic development occurs" (2 S).

Such standing up for a different view was exactly what Jung had asked Schmid to do when he cast Schmid in the role of the extravert in the dialogue. That this led to a formulation that today sounds very much like that of object relations is entirely consistent with Jung's notion of how the extravert relates to the object, with interest and engagement over time, seeing such a relation as a process of development. When Jung refrains from mirroring Schmid, he is not being patronizing to Schmid but tells him just what he thinks, and even what he has already thought, in a way that draws away from privileging Schmid as a source of insight. Jung is playing—as he himself says, "hypothetically"—the part of the introvert, not admitting easily to common ground but repeatedly asserting first principles derived from an internal standard of truth. Most strikingly, Jung refuses almost all of Schmid's attempts to reach an understanding on extraverted, feeling grounds. (At this early point in the development of the theory of types that they are attempting to explore, extraversion was equated with feeling, and introversion with thinking, and these terms had acquired neither the differentiation nor the technical meanings that would be assigned them in *Psychological Types*.)

The model of the psyche the men were using in 1915 to ground their discussion included not just the two psychological types that, to the exclusion of each other, would govern an individual conscious attitude, but a recognition of the unconscious, in which the other attitude would be present in an inferior, less developed form. Both men had trained as psychiatrists, were depth psychotherapists, and considered themselves colleagues because they were fellow analysts in the Zurich School of Analytical Psychology, which meant that they practiced an ethic of honesty in their exchanges with each other that included their direct emotional reactions. It was entirely in keeping with this convention that Jung, even when representing a hypothetical thinking standpoint, would express his *feeling* about the way the conversation was going, and that he sometimes did so in testy ways, reflecting the "inferior" extraversion (and feeling) that went with the territory of the thinking type he was playing in the dialogue. Similarly, for Schmid to use extended metaphors to convey what he *thought* about the type problem was quite in keeping with the image-based thinking that was supposed to characterize the unconscious of the more feeling-oriented extravert. The dialogue between the men therefore includes not only a directed exposition by each of the conscious standpoint of the type he has agreed to represent but also a more dramatic enactment of that type's unconscious aspect.[30] One of their early disagreements, for instance, concerns whether Schmid really understands that Jung, when describing how he thinks, is not conveying personal opinions: "I did not express any personal conviction with this description, nor did I want to convey an expression of my personal opinion through it, but I was thinking *hypothetically*" (3 J).

Jung is saying this because he believes a misunderstanding has developed (with Schmid) since the extravert is "inclined to understand such an expression in a concrete way." Schmid protests at the outset of his very next communication: "I did not take your remarks in the first letter as an expression of your personal statement. I contrasted your hypothetical think-

[30] The distinction between directed thinking as a modality of consciousness and "undirected" or "merely associative" thinking as a modality of the unconscious, had been put forward by Jung (influenced by William James) in 1911, two years before his first paper on psychological types (cf. Jung 1911/12, part I, chap. 2).

ing with my hypothetical feeling in hypothesizing that your remarks were your personal conviction. I reacted to this hypothesis, but I was well aware of the fact that it was only a hypothesis. I find it absolutely mandatory that we should give each other the credit to assume that neither of us wants to react in a personal way against the other; but we must, in order to get spontaneous reactions, adopt the attitude that each of us writes *as if* the one would think in this way, and the other feel in this way" (4 S).

Evidently, each of them feels free, in the course of playing his role in the dialogue, to speak from the area of his superiority to the relative inferiority of the other's thinking or feeling. Reading the dialogue with an understanding of the totality of what they are trying to represent to each other, both the conscious and unconscious sides of the characters they are personifying, it is impressive how well the two men play their roles. It is therefore a bit perplexing to experience their mutual frustration at the dialogue, which does not seem to allow either man fully to appreciate the integrity with which the other is representing the standpoint he agreed to represent. Instead, by the time the dialogue comes to an end, it seems to reach an impasse that leads each man to exit it by simply asserting a different model of the psyche.

Within this exchange, Schmid comes across as the more generous with symbolic images that he thinks can transcend such a standoff, and Jung more insistent about establishing principles and inner facts before any meeting of their different minds can even be contemplated.[31] There is, however, another issue between them besides epistemology, namely, an element of unresolved transference. In the seventh letter of this corre-

[31] Deirdre Bair even finds that "Schmid expressed his views with a maturity that made Jung, by contrast, seem juvenile, aggressive, and unfair" (2003, p. 279). I would argue, rather, that Jung comes across as unafraid to show an avuncular stance toward Schmid, one that we sense he fully expects Schmid to refuse, and thus is offering his friend every opportunity to declare his own standpoint and his freedom from all external influence, including Jung's. Such a stance, however, makes the correspondence more flattering to Schmid than to Jung.

spondence (7 J), Jung hints at the fact that Schmid had been his analytic patient and that there had been a significant misunderstanding between them when they were working together: "You have witnessed a famous case of this kind, in which a distinguished extravert was put, by an introvert *de pur sang*, into the saddle that is so characteristic of the extravert, on which he then galloped off to those adventures in which he learned to 'realize.' This was not taught to him. He learned it by himself because he had no other choice."

Later in the same letter, Jung adds: "Since I cannot provide you with evidence from my ongoing analyses, as you know nothing about them, I must revert to that famous case mentioned above, in which you have witnessed my method—which you seem to refer to in your letter—put into practice. The relation to the object that resulted from that analysis seems to have had a not inconsiderable influence on the further course the development of this extravert took. He has often been heard talking of Tristan and Iseult, of Faust and Helen, etc."

As Schmid had mentioned Tristan and Iseult as well as Faust as recently as his previous letter of the dialogue (6 S), it is Schmid that Jung is referring to. Jung is reminding Schmid that he has witnessed Jung's method directly because he was once Jung's analysand; the "famous case" that opened the door to an extraverted type's development was that of Schmid himself, with Jung as the analyst. The discussion of type, then, is being used by Jung to define the nature of their therapeutic interaction—and to remind Schmid that Jung is not as misunderstanding of what relationship to the object means to Schmid as the latter might imagine.

Schmid, for his part, is able, in the next letter (8 S), to report that he has engaged in an introspective way with Jung's suggestion that there is an element of unresolved transference in his refusal to acknowledge that Jung does know what it means to love an object:

> I have submitted to that famous extravert, as you call him, the remarks you made about him, and you might perhaps

be interested in hearing what he had to say about them. He is grateful to the introvert *de pur sang* for having allowed him complete freedom in his development, and for not having forced him, for example, to remain sitting in the saddle on which he had put him. He acknowledges that this effort is particularly deserving of thanks. He denies, however, that he was sitting in the saddle on which the introvert had put him when he galloped away to those adventures, as you put it. He maintains that he was not able to advance even one single step toward the realization of his feelings so long as he remained sitting in this saddle, and felt compelled to abandon some, then more, and finally practically all views about relations with the object he had taken over from the introvert *de pur sang*, particularly the view on the subjective plane, which was an obstacle to the realization of his feelings. Only after he had discarded everything that had been between him and the horse was he able to 'gallop away,' and only then could he find a saddle that fitted his own and the horse's nature.

This is a remarkable passage. It makes clear that (a) Schmid, during his analysis, had understood the need to disidentify with Jung, (b) Jung was already by 1915 engaged with discussions of "relations with the object" with his patients, and (c) both men found it necessary, after the period of their formal work, to clarify the process of separation of their natures that had taken place during Schmid's psychotherapy.

The letters thus give a rare glimpse of a process that is seldom complete at the time of "termination" of analysis, the resolution of a transference relationship. That Jung feels the process is complete after Schmid has expressed his view of what transpired between them is evidenced by the fact that he now feels able to bring the correspondence to an end. His next letter to Schmid is called "The last one," and in it he chooses to simplify the feeling ground that has in fact been covered when he says that "the point seems to be precisely that we don't agree." As if to underline that he will no longer be working with Schmid on the question of psychological types, Jung closes this letter with a unilateral move: outlining in meticulous detail where he thinks type theory is at the end of 1915. He includes important additions to the theory that have not previously been covered in the correspondence. Although it has seemed up to now that "intuition" has received scant attention in these letters, given its importance to Jung's later type theory, here Jung takes pains to make clear that he now sees intuition as the guiding principle of the unconscious. Therefore, the relatively unconscious thinking of the feeling type and feeling of the thinking type both operated intuitively.

This understanding that in the unconscious thinking (and, by analogy, feeling) will have an irrational basis carries forward the assertion Jung sets forth in the first chapter of *Wandlungen und Symbole der Libido*, that there are two kinds of thinking—one for the conscious, which is directed thinking guided by rational principles of logic and judgement, and one for the unconscious, which is undirected and carried forward by symbols (cf. Jung, 1911/12, §§ 15–50). At the time he wrote this letter to Schmid, Jung had not yet been convinced by Maria Moltzer that intuition could also be a conscious function. However, the way he stresses that intuition, though irrational, can yet be a potential source of new understanding—the thinking and feeling of the future—seems to reflect what he has learned in the course of the active imaginations recorded in *Liber Novus*. There, as we now know, he had written that "my soul gave me ancient things that pointed to the future. She gave me three things: The misery of war, the darkness of magic, and the gift of religion" (Jung, 2009, p. 306). All these irrational sources of insight are intuitive ways the unconscious has of informing the conscious mind.

For the most part, Jung's understanding of *conscious* functioning remains little altered from what he had presented to the Munich Psychoanalytic Congress in his paper on psychological types (1913a), read three months before his active imaginations began: two years later, he still regards feeling as the guiding conscious process for the extraverted type and thinking as the guiding process for the introverted type. It is in the correspondence with Schmid, however, that Jung first identifies the feeling of the feeling type as a *rational* function, breaking ranks with many earlier psychologists who had tended to see feeling as irrational, because derived from emotion as opposed to reason. Jung makes it clear that he sees any imputation of irrationality to feeling as applying only to the unconscious feeling of the thinking type, thus entitling the feeling type extravert the same claim to rationality as the thinking type introvert.

There are a few signs in the last letter (9 J) that he has started to think of sensation as a third function operating in consciousness. Jung's linking the term "sensation" with "organ function" suggests that his notion of sensation at this time was that it was equivalent to a body sense, or what he would later call "introverted sensation." When he goes on to speak, in part IV of the outline statement contained in this letter, of "acting (experience via the object)" as a way to assimilate the unconscious, Jung may be making his first stab at formulating what he would later, in *Psychological Types*, describe as belonging to "extraverted sensation" (Jung, 1921, § 604: "Sensation, in the extraverted attitude, is pre-eminently conditioned by the object"; § 605: "As sensation is chiefly conditioned by the object, those objects that excite the strongest sensations will be decisive for the individual's psychology"; and § 606: "This type—the majority appear to be men—naturally does not think he is at the 'mercy' of sensation. He would ridicule this point of view as quite beside the point, because sensation for him is a concrete expression of life—it is simply real life lived to the full"). Although his 1915 formulation of "experience via the object" could be read as if the "object" were typically an outer one being engaged with in an extraverted way, the active quality of the imaginations he was recording in the *Red Book*, in which he observed and interacted with his fantasy figures as real, may have played the decisive role in his recognition of the necessity of "action" to "assimilate the unconscious."

This outline statement of what Jung thought the types were in 1915, then, can be directly compared with Jung's earlier comment (1913a) to see the distance the theory had come in two short years, and we can also compare it to a subsequent statement (Jung, 1921) to see how much farther he would take it after ending the correspondence with Schmid. Jung seems to have written this statement in 1915 to reclaim ownership of the theory. However, it was not the end of what Schmid had to say. This "last one" from Jung released a spate of new information from his former patient, who wrote no fewer than three more letters, to let Jung know about "what has been the most important work to me during the last months" (arguably his own Black Book) and, in a subsequent letter, to cough up at last some of the ways he felt his extraverted commitment to relationship (Eros) had been slighted, and even short-changed, by Jung's introverted stance as an analyst. Jung apparently did write back about that, as is evidenced by Schmid's references to Jung's reaction, although these communications appear to be lost.

The final two letters we have, both from Schmid, seem to me to complete his process of setting himself free, never more clearly than in these lines from 12 S (the letter of 17/18 December 1915) addressed, rather personally, to Jung: "Your reaction ... is a prime specimen of Mephistophelean wisdom. Its end provoked a laughter of relief, for which I heartily thank you.... I have an equally sharp-tongued Mephistopheles within myself, who showed me the same truths about God and the devil, Eros and the poisoner, etc. in an even more drastic manner already long ago, particularly in the black book."

Schmid is suggesting here that a process of introversion did occur for him in relation to this analysis, for he has kept his own black book of introverted experiences (just as Jung was doing during this period) and has found a similar part in himself to Jung's "Mephistopheles." As Schmid movingly puts it, "I know that I have always acknowledged, and will always acknowledge, in private and in public, in speech and in writing, the value of your thoughts; actually I also accepted your untruths at first, that is, also your devil. This was the only way it was possible for me to really acknowledge you.... I cannot understand why you distinguish so painstakingly between the moral and immoral, between divine and devilish love, in the extravert. They simply cannot be separated, because out of both—just as out of truth and untruth—the new develops again and again."

Thus it is hard to see this dialogue as ending simply in disagreement, and easy to imagine Jung having raised that possibility to give Schmid a chance to refute it. Both men come through as separate psychological individuals, and though their attempt at Platonic dialogue does end in a kind of stalemate that forces them to drop their typological masks, the friendship survived. Jung was invited to write the introduction to *Tag und Nacht*, the novel of introverted feeling and extraverted intuitive musings that Schmid eventually shared with the world. Upon Schmid's untimely death, Jung found himself able to write a generous obituary, which we have included as an appendix to this book. Schmid's daughter, Marie-Jeanne, became Jung's longtime secretary the following spring.

The Aftermath

(by Ernst Falzeder)

About a year after the end of his correspondence with Schmid, Jung wrote an important text, entitled *Die Psychologie der unbewußten Prozesse. Überblick über die moderne Theorie und Methode der analytischen Psychologie* [The psychology of unconscious processes. An overview of the modern theory and method of analytical psychology] (Jung, 1917a; finished in December 1916).[32] Its first part is an only slightly modified

[32] This was translated by Dora Hecht into English the same year under the title *The Psychology of the Unconscious Processes, Being a Survey of the Modern Theory and Method of Analytical Psychology*, and reprinted in the second edition of *Collected Papers on Analytical Psychology*, edited by Constance Long (Jung, 1917b). The versions of it contained in the GW and the CW, renamed *Über die Psychologie des Unbewussten* and *On the Psychology of the Unconscious* respectively, represent the final form the text took, as the second of Jung's *Two Essays on Analytical Psychology*, after two major revisions he made to it in 1925 and 1942. Translations from the original German text are my own.

reprint of a short popular article published in 1912, "New paths in psychology" (Jung, 1912) (in which typology is not mentioned). To this article he then added another ninety-five pages, however, in which he dealt with basic concepts of his own evolving psychology, including the question of psychological types. "He noted that it was a common development that the psychological characteristics of the types were pushed to extremes. By what he termed the law of enantiodromia, or the reversal into the opposite, the other function entered in, namely, feeling for the introvert, and thinking for the extravert. These secondary functions were found in the unconscious. The development of the contrary function led to individuation" (Shamdasani, in Jung, 2009, p. 210).

In general, Jung summarized his views as he had developed them in the exchange with Schmid. As in the correspondence, for instance, Jung continued to equate feeling(-into) with extraversion, and thinking with introversion.[33] (Interestingly, however, he already hinted at the possibility of further types: "I deliberately mention only these two types. Naturally, this does not exclude the possibility of the existence of other types. We know of still other possibilities" [Jung, 1917a, p. 77].) It sounds like an echo of his dispute with Schmid when Jung wrote that each of the types "speaks a different language," and that the quarrel between them "is venomous, violent, and full of mutual devaluations. For *the value of the one is the non-value of the other*" (ibid., p. 76). "Both devalue each other" (ibid., p. 59).[34] He again linked the conflict between the two types of personal psychology to the theories of Freud and Adler: "The sexual theory is a theory emanating from the feeling standpoint, while the power theory emanates from the

[33] As he also clearly stated in another text of 1916: "The introversion type knows only the thinking principle, the extraversion type only the feeling principle" (1916a, § 482).

[34] Cf. also the frequent references to the constant misunderstandings between the two types, and the tendency to devalue the other—no doubt also on the basis of his own experiences, not least in his relationship with Schmid—which run like a red thread through his descriptions in *Psychological Types* (chap. X).

thinking standpoint.... *both theories are the products of a one-sided psychology*" (ibid., p. 59; emphasis in original).

Some formulations and metaphors seem to have been taken directly from the correspondence, for example, when Jung wrote about those theories and methods: "In the hands of a good doctor ... both theories are beneficial *causticizers*, helpful in a dosage measured for the particular case, harmful and dangerous in a hand that does not know how to measure and to weigh. They are critical methods, which, like all criticisms, bring about something *good in cases where something may and must be destroyed*, dissolved, and reduced, but only do damage in any case where it is necessary to develop something.... both theories ... [are] like medicinal toxins" (ibid., pp. 60–61; emphasis added). This is reminiscent of the passage in Jung's letter to Schmid of 6 November 1915: "For ill people, 'analytical' understanding is as healingly destructive as *cauterization* or thermocautery, but healthy tissue is banefully destroyed by it. After all, it is a technique we learned from the devil, always destructive, but *useful where destruction is necessary*" (emphasis added).[35]

When did Jung stop linking introversion with thinking, and extraversion with feeling, and introduce sensation and intuition as two further functions? And who identified these latter functions? Jung expressly stated in *Psychological Types* that the "credit for having discovered the existence of this [intuitive] type belongs to Miss M. Moltzer" (1921, footnote to § 773). Moltzer had introduced it in two talks given before the Psychological Club in Zurich in 1916: "The tendency of individualisation also contains a collective element which arises in the half conscious, half unconscious function which we call intuition. Intuition ... contains elements of feelings as well as of thoughts, and tries to solve a given problem and

[35] We know about Freud's low opinion of this work from his dry reaction toward Abraham: "A woman patient of Jung's has sent me his new work on the psychology of the *Ucs.* so that I should change my judgment on the noble character. It bears the date 1917. But he seems not to have gone beyond the crude conversion into theory of the fact that he came across myself and Adler" (Freud & Abraham, 2002, p. 353).

create an adaptation in bringing together these half conscious and half unconscious elements. This adaptation coincides with neither the extraversion nor the introversion tendency—it contains elements of both. Therefore I am inclined to accept a third type which uses mainly this intuitive function in its adaptation to life" (Moltzer, 1916a, p. 109). In her second talk she added that she considered "intuition ... the oldest human function" that would have "grown out of instinct. I consider intuition to be the differentiation and the conscious function of instinct" (Moltzer, 1916b, pp. 116–17).[36]

Shamdasani comments that if "one compares Jung's concept of this type in *Psychological Types* with Moltzer's, it is apparent that their formulations, whilst overlapping, differ quite significantly.... it appears that Jung developed his concept of this type through extensively reworking Moltzer's concept, and recasting her trinitarian model into a quaternity" (Shamdasani, 1988b, p. 104), or rather, more specifically, through recasting Moltzer's trinitarian model of types into his concept of two *attitudes* and a quaternity of psychological *functions*.

In *Psychological Types*, Jung merely wrote that he had to realize, after thoroughly working through the material, "that we must treat the introverted and extraverted [attitude] types as categories over and above the function-types" (1921, § 836).[37] Jung's mature typology became possible only after he had clearly distinguished within types between *attitudes* and *functions* (1921, § 556), which were more or less independent of each other and could appear in any possible combination in a particular individual. In addition to thinking and

[36] In 1919 Jung gave a talk on "Instinct and the unconscious" (Jung, 1919), in which he compared instinct and intuition, in the following way: "It is a process analogous to instinct, with the difference that whereas instinct is a purposive impulse to carry out some highly complicated action, intuition is the unconscious, purposive apprehension of a highly complicated situation. In a sense, therefore, intuition is the reverse of instinct" (ibid., § 269).

[37] Cf. also the introduction: "A deeper study of the problem has shown this equation [i.e., introversion-thinking and extraversion-feeling] to be untenable" (1921, § 7); or a similar statement in ibid., § 248.

feeling, he introduced sensation (analogous to Janet's "fonction du réel") and finally, taking up and reworking Moltzer's suggestion, intuition as further psychological functions. Moreover, he distinguished between rational and irrational (or "aesthetic," in Nietzsche's term; cf. Jung, 1921, § 240) functions, which could then appear in a "superior" or "inferior" form in a particular case. New questions became possible: What function is used the most? Is it adjusted (and successful) or not? The use of what function leads to unfavorable outcomes? In this way, the typology evolved into a system of coordinates for the practical use of the psychologist or psychotherapist, going beyond a mere characterology or a superficial a priori classification.

This conceptualization must have taken place sometime between December 1916 (when he finished his monograph on the unconscious processes, in which the duality introversion-thinking and extraversion-feeling was still upheld) and October 1919 at the latest, when his final model was already fully developed. Although the manuscript of *Psychological Types* was finished only in the spring of 1920,[38] the main body of the work had been completed earlier. Hannah noted that "all the research and most of the writing was done during the war" (1976, p. 134). This is confirmed by a letter Jung wrote to Smith Ely Jelliffe in August 1917, while on military duty in Chateau d'Oex: "As soon as I am back again, I try to finish a rather long paper about the types" (in Burnham, 1983, p. 199). By December, he was able to tell Sabina Spielrein that "you are an intuitive extravert type" (letter dated 18 December 1917 in Covington & Wharton, 2003, p. 52). We also know that in "1918, he presented a series of seminars to the Psychological Club on his work on typology, and was engaged in extensive scholarly research on this subject" (Shamdasani, in Jung, 2009, p. 210). Obviously, he had already developed the full eightfold typological schema and already finished at least a draft of this book, on 7 October 1919, when he wrote

[38] This is the date of the preface, and Jung "always dated his prefaces when he had finished the book" (Hannah, 1976, p. 134).

to Spielrein: "I cannot answer your question about types. I would have to write a book about it. *Actually it has already been written*. Your questions are answered there in detail. When I wrote it I had to cancel out the fundamental identity of extraversion and feeling, and of introversion and thinking. That was wrongly conceived and came from the fact that introverted thinking types and extraverted feeling types are the most conspicuous" (in Covington & Wharton, 2003, p. 57; emphasis added). He also sent her a diagram, in which he gave the positions of himself, Bleuler, Freud, and Nietzsche with reference to thinking, feeling, sensation, and intuition (ibid.).

In 1920, Jung gave his reason for not including the present exchange in *Psychological Types*: "The correspondence belongs essentially to the preparatory stage of the work, and its inclusion would create more confusion than clarity" (1921, p. xii). Now, nearly a century later, it is to be hoped that the first publication of these letters in English,[39] in a scholarly, annotated edition, will not "create more confusion than clarity," but instead will shed more light on the development of Jung's theory of types, particularly on the co-construction of that theory in the dialogue with Hans Schmid-Guisan.

[39] So far, only two somewhat longer passages have been reprinted in English, both from letter 9 J (Jung, 1973b, pp. 30–32; van der Post, 1976, pp. 123–24).

Translator's Note

Any translation requires a compromise between the imperative to retain, as much as possible, the literal meaning along with the characteristic peculiarities of the original, and the need to render it in idiomatic English and avoid "translationese." There always remain cases of doubt, however, in which I have opted for a translation close to the German original rather than for fluency in contemporary English.

A case in point would be *Einfühlung*, a perfectly common and ordinary term in German, for which there is no exact equivalent in English. Rather than using "empathy" to translate it, for example, I have decided on "feeling-into," unusual as it may sound. This is not only a literal translation but also the term chosen by H. Godwin Baynes in the first English translation of Jung's *Psychological Types* (London: Routledge & Kegan Paul, 1923). Since Baynes, who lived in Zurich at the time, was assisted in the translation by Jung himself, who listened "to my translation week by week ... offering invaluable suggestions" (Baynes, in Jung, 1921[1923], p. xxi), we may be certain that the choice of this word met with the latter's approval, or might even have been suggested by him. Moreover, "feeling-into" also preserves the associative closeness this term has in Jung's theory with the psychological function of *Fühlen* or "feeling."

In another instance, a term that was and still is commonplace in German vernacular speech, *Persönlichkeit* (which can mean character, figure, identity, individual, personage, personality, personhood), has taken on, in its literal translation "personality," further specific meanings, particularly in psychology, that it would be hard to assume Jung and Schmid had in mind in 1915. Even so, I have chosen "personality" because the alternatives would probably have been even more open to misunderstandings. I should add that this was also the choice of James Strachey et al. in their translation of Sigmund Freud's works, thus setting a precedent in translations in depth psychology.

The way the term "object" is used in this correspondence is, so to speak, a residue of the psychoanalytic vocabulary, where it stands for the object of a desire or drive, hence not necessarily for an inanimate thing, but most often for another person—rather in the manner of such everyday English expressions as "love object" or "the object of my affection."

A word might be appropriate regarding both writers' usage of terms that today are regarded by many as insensitive if not incorrect, such as "Negro," or "he," "his," "man," "mankind," etc., when used as generic terms for both sexes. Nevertheless, I found it important to leave that usage—which the writers and their contemporaries took for granted—unchanged, lest ending up "doctoring" the original. Any text bears the hallmarks of the era in which it was written. So instead of rewriting a text that is almost one hundred years old according to Western standards of the second decade of the twenty-first century, I ask the reader to bear in mind its historical context.

Although these letters may have been written with an eye on a possible future publication, they are still personal, handwritten letters, and not a text that has been repeatedly gone through, checked, proofread, and so forth, for print. Occasionally, phrases are obscure even in the original German, there are stylistic slip-ups, reiterations of words, grammatical mistakes, and so on. Here, too, I have not tried to "improve" on the original by correcting these inaccuracies but rather have sought to render them faithfully in the translation, thereby preserving the atmosphere of this epistolary exchange.

Many of Jung's terms—from the archetypes to the collective unconscious, from the midlife crisis to his theory of complexes, and of course his typology of introverts and extraverts—have become household names. In the process of being absorbed into everyday language, however, some of these terms and concepts have been garbled or distorted, including their correct spelling. Contemporary spell-checking programs, for instance, autocorrect Jung's etymologically correct expression "extr*a*version" into "extr*o*version." All authoritative English dictionaries I consulted, in print or online, give "extr*o*vert(ed)" as the standard form (both for American and British English), while listing "extr*a*vert(ed)" only as a variant. Still, I have stubbornly retained the term as coined by Jung, who himself underlined that "extr*o*vert is bad Latin and should not be used" (in McGuire & Hull, 1977, p. 213).

Contrary to modern American usage, by the way, I have also retained the original full spelling of words such as "acknowledg*e*ment" or "judg*e*ment." Whether or not one agrees with Sir James Murray's opinion that dropping the *e* "is against all analogy, etymology, and orthoepy," and that one "ought to set a scholarly example, instead of following the ignorant to do ill" (*Hart's Rules for Compositors and Readers at the University Press Oxford*, 39th ed., 1983, p. 86), keeping the *e* in used to be the standard form, and certainly was in the era of this correspondence.

It remains to gratefully acknowledge the support and assistance in preparing this translation of my coeditor John Beebe, John Burnham, Esther Moises, and Sonu Shamdasani, as well as of the community of the translators' forum at http://dict.leo.org/forum. Special thanks go to Tony Woolfson for yet another excellent and fruitful collaboration on bringing out more of the "unknown Jung" in the English language.

Ernst Falzeder
Salzburg, August 2011

Correspondence

1 J

[4 June 1915]

Dear Friend,

As you know from our previous talks, for the past few years I have occupied myself with the question of psychological types,[40] a problem as difficult as it is interesting. What originally led me to that problem were not intellectual presuppositions, but actual difficulties in my daily analytical work with my patients, as well as experiences I have had in my personal relations with other people. You remember that our earlier discussions about certain controversial points of analytical psychology,[41] too, seemed to point, in our view, to the existence of two diametrically opposed types.[42] At the time we took great pains to put the typical differences into words and, in so doing, discovered not only the extraordinary difficulty of such a project but also its tremendous importance for the psychology of human relations in general. Step by step, we realized that the scope of this problem took on extraordinary dimensions, so that, as is always the case in such situations, we somewhat lost courage and the hope that the problem could be dealt with at all.

For one thing we saw very clearly: the problem is not so much the intellectual difficulty of formulating the differences between the types in a logical way, but rather the acceptance of a viewpoint that is diametrically opposed to our own, and which essentially forces the problem of the *existence of two kinds of truth* upon us.[43] Thus we arrived at a critical point of

[40] On the development of Jung's thoughts on the question of psychological types prior to this correspondence, see the introduction.

[41] On "analytical psychology," see the introduction, note 22.

[42] It is unclear when exactly these earlier discussions had taken place. They probably played a role in Schmid's analysis with Jung (see the introduction and below).

[43] This goes beyond Jung (1913a), where he had asserted only that in psychology these two types had led to the two different theories of Freud and Adler.

the greatest order, because we had to ask ourselves, in all seriousness, whether the existence of two kinds of truth is conceivable at all. Since we are both not professional philosophers, but at best mere dilettantes[44] (and, being dilettantes, we *love* philosophy, in contrast to the professionals who *practice* it), this was a nearly hopeless problem for us, because viewing the world in the light of two truths seemed at least a highly daring acrobatic feat to us, for which our brains, insufficiently trained in this specialty, were hardly adequate.

I do not know how you have tried to come to terms with this. I would guess that you, true to your character, have simply gone ahead with your life, assuming that everybody can have his own personal views, views that can freely lead their own separate existence without disturbing the harmony of the world mechanism, even if they are not in accordance with other views. But as I am one of those people who must a priori always have a viewpoint before being able to enter into something, I could not be reassured by simply going ahead in my personal relations; to allay my concerns, I needed the points of view provided by the *pragmatic movement* in modern philosophy. Although I make no secret of my highest esteem for someone like *Schiller*[45] or *William James*,[46] I also have to confess that prag-

[44] Manuscript [MS]: *Dilettanten*. Here used in a nonpejorative sense, that is, referring to amateurs, not professionally trained philosophers,.

[45] Ferdinand Canning Scott Schiller (1864–1937), the primary English representative of pragmatism at this time. In his *Studies in Humanism*, he had defined the principles of pragmatism as follows: (1) "truths are logical values," (2) "the 'truth' of an assertion depends on its application," (3) "the meaning of a rule lies in its application," (4) "all meaning depends on purpose," (5) "all mental life is purposive," pragmatism must become (6) "a systematic protest against all ignoring of the purposiveness of actual knowing," and as such it can be described as (7) "a conscious application to epistemology or logic of a teleological psychology, which implies, ultimately, a voluntaristic metaphysic" (2nd ed. 1912, reprint 2008, pp. 49–52).

[46] William James (1841–1910), the famous American psychologist and philosopher. The basic notion of pragmatism, according to James, is to trace the "concrete consequence" of each of our beliefs (1907, p. 49; 1975 ed., p. 30). He had differentiated between the "tender-minded" rationalists and the "tough-minded" empiricists. "[H]e proposed pragmatism as a philosophy that could satisfy both types" of approach to life and resolve the different viewpoints "through invoking the pragmatic rule" and "weighing up the resul-

matism leaves me with a somewhat stale feeling. I cannot help it: it is a bit "business-like."[47] It is a bit like my feelings concerning the saying, *ubi bene, ibi patria*,[48] which I have never much liked either. As I belong to that category of people who never take the element of feeling sufficiently into account, as opposed to the intellect, it was necessary that I should not neglect to also ask my feeling for its opinion in this matter. A man of your kind, however, who is as much devoted to feeling as I am to the intellect, comes to the help, not of the intellect, but of the feeling in the other. And that is why it is to a thinker who probably belongs to your type—namely, the romantic, as *Ostwald*[49] called him—to whom I owe a notion that freed me from that certain staleness of pragmatism. It was *Bergson* who gave me the notion of the *irrational*.[50] What I like is the unmistakable

---

tant practical implications of each position" (Shamdasani, 2003, p. 60; cf. Goodman, 1995, p. 55). Jung had first met James at Clark University in 1909 and paid him a visit the following year. In an unpublished chapter of *Memories, Dreams, Reflections*, he states that they had had an "excellent rapport," "that James was one of the most outstanding persons that he had ever met," and that he became "a model" for him (in Shamdasani, 2003, p. 58). On James and Jung, see also Taylor, 1980.

[47] The expression is in English in the original. For instance, James had famously written of "truth's cash-value" (1907, p. 200).

[48] The Latin is translated as, "Where I am at ease, there is my fatherland."

[49] Wilhelm Ostwald (1853–1932), Latvian-born physical chemist, Nobel Prize for Chemistry in 1909. In his popular book, *Große Männer* [*Great Men*] (1909), he "makes the attempt to classify scientific men of genius and to formulate the laws governing their careers," by dividing them into two types, the romanticists and the classicists. The classicists have "a low reaction velocity," developing their ideas slowly and alone, with the result that the creativity of their contribution is usually recognized late, and the romanticists "a high one," creating, through their enthusiasm for their own ideas, a large early following of associates and champions (Bancroft, 1910, p. 91). See also Simmer (1978) for a discussion of Ostwald's typology.

[50] In *Creative Evolution*, a work that attracted a wide popular following for the French philosopher Henri Bergson (1859–1941), the irrational is introduced under the notion of "disorder." Bergson speaks of the need to include disorder in our mathematical models of how the universe is ordered, demonstrating that if we do so, we soon notice two kinds of order: willed order and the chaotic or capricious order dictated by chance, which is what we are referring to when we speak of "disorder" (Bergson, 1907, chap. 3). Jung held Bergson in high esteem. He remarked on 20 March 1914, that

hypostasization[51] of this notion. As a consequence we get two intimately connected, mutually dependent principles: the *rational* and the *irrational*.[52] It gives me pleasure to think of them as hypostatic, because then I can acknowledge their existence also morally. I think you will understand that I do not practice philosophy here but rather make psychological confessions to you, which cannot hurt even the specialist, because in psychology thoughts are toll free, being psychology themselves. We have long ceased to pride ourselves that we could rise above psychology by thinking. This latter viewpoint is one of the medieval privileges of our academies, hallowed by their venerable age. The Archimedean point outside of psychology, with the help of which we would be able to unhinge psychology, is hardly likely to be found.[53]

So (naturally) I called my viewpoint rational, and the viewpoint opposed to mine irrational. Thus, your viewpoint fell into the category of the irrational. As the irrational cannot be further understood at all, I came to the conclusion that one truth must remain unintelligible to the other. With this, I drew a thick line between you and me, because I also said to myself: you are as irrational to me as I am irrational to you. This would

---

"Bergson ... says everything that we have not said" (Minutes of the Association for Analytical Psychology, Psychological Club, Zurich, vol. 1, p. 57). A few months later, he noted that his own "constructive method" corresponded to Bergson's "intuitive method" (in Jung, 1917b, p. 399). In a paper of 1916, Jung again underlined that "[w]e are particularly indebted to Bergson for having taken up the cudgels for the irrational's right to exist" (1916a, § 483). Jung possessed the 1912 German translation of *L'évolution creatrice*.

[51] Hypostasis, literally "that which stands beneath": substance, basis; essential nature or underlying reality. Hypostasization: reification, objectification of a notion that exists only in the mind.

[52] The terms "rational" and "irrational" are not yet being used here as they would be in Jung's later typology, although his acknowledgement later in the letter that the feeling standpoint is also rational from the feeling person's perspective is a step toward his eventual view that both thinking and feeling are "rational" functions (and sensation and intuition "irrational" ones).

[53] "Give me a place to stand on, and I will move the Earth," Archimedes is said to have exclaimed while analyzing the principle of the lever. Throughout his work, Jung stressed the importance of the fact that, in psychology, the observer and the observed coincide. See the introduction and note 24.

create a definitive but hopeless situation, satisfying for the intellect but depressing for the feeling. In this situation, I remembered that we are in possession of a very nice analytical method, which we use every day with our patients, and the excellent results of which basically consist in bringing together and balancing the antagonistic forces in the human soul, so that even the antagonism, which previously had an inhibiting effect, becomes a step leading one up in life.

Thus, when one of my patients dreams of a Herr Müller and then tells me during the analysis that this Herr Müller is a very disagreeable person, cantankerous in his moods and mudslinging, that he has always meddled with the patient's life in a most annoying way, just like his father, who, overzealously concerned about his education, used to come between the patient and his wishes—I would say: "Sure it's like that. You see, there are lots of people who do not achieve self-realization but always unload their demands and their own fantasies and fantasized wishes onto others, and get on their nerves, instead of minding their own business. Herr Müller is a good example of this kind, and so is your father, bless his soul. But why are you still irritated by this? After all, you are not married to Herr Müller, and your father has been dwelling in Elysium for nearly twenty years, from where he can hardly be expected to exert an annoying influence on the upper world. Unless, that is, his imago,[54] the image of his memory in

[54] A term first introduced by Jung in the first part of *Transformations and Symbols of the Libido*. There he stated that the name was taken from the title of a novel (1906) by the Swiss writer Carl Spitteler, and from the ancient religious idea of *imagines et lares* (images/statues and tutelary gods of home/hearth) (1911/12, German ed., p. 164; also in CW 5, § 62 and note 5). In his Fordham Lectures in September 1912, he specified that a patient's "love, admiration, resistance, hatred and rebelliousness still cling to the effigies" of the parents long after the latter have departed. "It was this fact that compelled me to speak no longer of 'father' and 'mother' but to employ instead the term 'imago,' because these fantasies are not concerned any more with the real father and mother but with subjective and often very distorted images of them" (Jung, 1913b, § 305). Also in 1912, Freud founded *Imago, Journal for the Application of Psychoanalysis to the Humanities*, equally named after Spitteler's novel. The concept of "imago" in Jung's sense was quickly and widely adopted in psychoanalytic circles.

your fantasy, is still active. This effect is strongly reminiscent of that of a posthypnotic suggestion. But do you know which suggestions are most effective? Precisely those that suit us, even though we don't always like to admit it. If suggestions, simply as such, were effective, as many people believe, the suggestion therapy of neuroses would really be a panacea. We have learned that this is not so, however. So both the imago and Herr Müller suit you very well, which is indeed annoying. In other words: they are apt expressions of one side of your personality, which you do not want to see. That is why you are irritated by the mote in your brother's eye but not by the beam in your own eye."[55]

As you know, we call this second viewpoint the interpretation of a dream on the subjective plane, while the first viewpoint, as outlined above, corresponds to an interpretation on the objective plane.[56] Both viewpoints are in accord with the truth. Actually these are two truths, two different, but equally

[55] Matthew 7:1–5.

[56] Jung first mentioned the principle of dream interpretation on the subjective plane or level, without yet calling it so, in 1910 in "Psychic conflicts in a child" (an article based on a talk he had given at the Clark University Conference in 1909): "The principal protagonist in the dream is always the dreamer himself" (Jung, 1910, § 39). The first explicit mentioning of this distinction in the literature seems to be Alphonse Maeder's talk at the Munich Congress in 1913 (the same, at which Jung delivered his paper on psychological types; see the introduction), in which Maeder expressly attributed this "excellent expression" and notion to Jung (Maeder, 1913, pp. 11, 13). Jung himself spoke about this in a discussion of dream interpretation on 30 January 1914, in the Zurich "Psychoanalytic Society (Society for Analytical Psychology)," at which Schmid was probably present (he contributed to the discussion when it was continued in the following session): On the subjective plane the "dream images do not reflect the relations between the dreamer and the persons seen in the dream, but they are an expression of tendencies within the dreamer" (*Protokolle* etc., 1913–16; our translation). Cf. the definitions in *Psychological Types*: "When I speak of interpreting a dream or fantasy on the objective level, I mean that the persons or situations appearing in it are referred to objectively as real persons or situations" (1921, § 779). "When I speak of interpreting a dream or fantasy on the subjective level, I mean that the persons or situations appearing in it refer to subjective factors entirely belonging to the subject's own psyche" (ibid., § 812). In this letter Jung links introversion with a tendency to interpret on the subjective plane, and extraversion with a tendency to interpret on the objective plane.

true, perceptions of one and the same situation. One truth says: it is he, while the other says: it is also I (but I do not want to see it).

I wrote above: you are irrational. But if I think analytically, I will say: and so am I (but I do not want to see it). For the rational is what is given in my consciousness, and what is comprehensible, while the irrational is what is present in my unconscious, and what is incomprehensible. Insofar as you, in accordance with your character, represent the feeling standpoint, while I call your standpoint irrational, I am actually projecting a judgement, which holds true only for me. You regard your feeling standpoint as rational; I regard my thinking standpoint as rational. But as I hold the thinking standpoint, I am not at the same time consciously holding the feeling standpoint, which for me, as a consequence, does not fall into the category of the rational but is of necessity irrational. For the same reasons, for you the thinking standpoint falls into the category of the irrational, because for you rationality is tied to the feeling standpoint. As is easily imaginable, the greatest misunderstandings may arise out of this situation, and, as you know, they actually did arise, and how! These are instructive experiences for those whose friendship withstands the heaviest blows, but sources of bitterness for those who are never able to yield to a different standpoint but always just accuse the others of not being able to yield themselves.

You will perhaps find it strangely intellectual when I tell you that I got rid of these difficulties by viewing things on the subjective plane. In this way I was able to realize that a different standpoint, which I cannot but call irrational, seems to be irrational only because this same standpoint is irrational in myself. For you it may be absolutely rational, however. I think this fact can be explained as follows: a person with intellectual abilities instinctively prefers to adjust to the object by way of thinking (abstraction), whereas a person whose feeling exceeds his intellectual abilities prefers to adjust to the object by way of feeling himself into[57] the object. This results in the

[57] MS: *Einfühlung*.

rational quality of thinking in the former, and the rational quality of feeling in the latter. Owing to the preference of thinking, feeling-into will remain in a relatively undeveloped state and will thus function in an irregular, unpredictable, and uncontrollable way—in one word, irrationally.[58] Naturally man, ever mindful of his role as *Homo sapiens*, tries to tame and control the irrational with the rational. As a consequence, the thinking person wants to force his feeling to serve his thinking, and the feeling person his thinking to serve his feeling. When I see this done by other people, it strikes me as completely absurd, because the other person does the very thing that most runs counter to my ideal. I call it childish and twisted. It is nearly impossible for me not to moralize about it. The stronger my ideal is, and the more I cherish it, the more I actually have to condemn the other, because he acts contrary to my ideal—which I naturally consider to be *the* ideal. After all, I want to purge my thinking of all that is erratic and unaccountable, of all pleasure and unpleasure caused by personal feeling, and raise it to the height of justness and the crystal-clear purity of the universally valid idea, way beyond anything connected with mere feeling. You, on the contrary, want to put your feeling above your personal thinking, and to free it from all the fantasized and infantile thoughts that might impede its development. That is why the thinking person represses his all-embracing feeling, and the feeling person his all-embracing thinking. But the thinking person accepts feelings that correspond to his thinking, and the feeling person accepts thoughts that correspond to his feeling.

The two of them speak different languages, so that they often cannot understand each other at all. I even suspect that the thinking person speaks of feeling when he is actually thinking, and the feeling person of thinking when he is feeling. It is certain, however, that what the feeling person calls thinking is just a *representation*[59] but not an abstraction. His ap-

[58] These formulations foreshadow Jung's later differentiation between "superior" and "inferior" functions (cf. Jung, 1921; Definitions: Inferior Function).

[59] MS: *ein Vorstellen.*

proach to thinking is therefore extraordinarily concretistic, and it is immediately noticeable that it cannot turn into an abstraction. Vice versa, the feeling of the thinking person is not at all what the feeling person would call feeling, but is really a *sensation*,[60] as a rule of a reactive nature, and thus very concretistic, if not to say "physiological."

I am leaving out here something we will have to discuss later.

With best regards,
your Jung

[60] MS: *eine Empfindung*.

2 S

[24 June 1915]

Dear Friend,

As you have guessed, dealing further with the question of the psychological types has not given me any real headaches. I have never been fainthearted or desperate, but in finding similar opposites in the most varied fields I have tried to find the consolation that development is not possible at all without opposites. I have never viewed the problem of the types as the existence of two truths, however, but I have rather envisaged, from the genetic point of view, the existence of two poles between which psychic development occurs.

When I read Bergson's "*Évolution créatrice*" [*Creative Evolution*] two years ago, I tried to draw parallels between the urge toward abstraction and the urge toward feeling-into, on the one hand, and Bergson's pairs of opposites: plant and animal life on the one side, and intellect and instinct, on the other.[61] If life is always built upon the interplay between complementary, yet also diverging, tendencies, why shouldn't this also be the case in psychology? Like Bergson, I conceived the opposites as springing from a common primordial type that originally united both tendencies in itself.[62] As development progresses, everybody is following only one tendency and lets the other atrophy. If opposites develop in this process, it is still their *purpose* to complement each other. Just as the cycle

[61] Bergson explores these branchings of life energy throughout chapter 2 of his book, concluding that "consciousness, after having been obliged, in order to set itself free, to divide organization into two complementary parts, vegetables on one hand and animals on the other, has sought an issue in the double direction of instinct and of intelligence" (Bergson, 1907, p. 185).

[62] Bergson speaks of "the dissociation of the primordial tendency into such and such complementary tendencies which create divergent lines of evolution" (ibid., p. 255).

of the content of carbonic acid and oxygen[63] in the atmosphere is maintained by the antagonism of plant and animal life, I envisage that psychic development is made possible only by an antagonism between feeling-into and abstraction. "L'évolution ... ne s'accomplit jamais dans le sens d'une association, mais d'une dissociation, jamais vers la convergence, mais vers la divergence des efforts."[64] In doing this, I have always tried to keep clearly in mind that the tendencies, into which the primordial tendency split, must be of equal value, for Bergson also writes: "Il faut que les éléments, en lesquels une tendance se dissocie aient la même importance et surtout la même puissance d'évoluer." However: "on est tenté d'y voir des activités dont la première serait supérieure à la seconde et s'y superposerait, alors qu'en réalité ce ne sont pas chose de même ordre ni qui se soient succédé l'une à l'autre, ni auxquelles on puisse assigner des rangs."[65] Thus I, too, have been tempted time and again to see your standpoint as irrational, and mine as the only rational one. And it has taken me some time to realize that I am mistaken in having believed that everybody else would have to go to heaven in my own way.

I had no fear that through the knowledge of diametrically opposed types "the harmony of the world mechanism would be disturbed." I rather took the view that dissonance is a *conditio sine qua non* of all harmony. But neither do I believe that the two types can lead an undisturbed *existence of their own*. Harmony is possible only when *different* tones sound together. I envisage harmony as being the result of a gradual process in

[63] Corrected from *Kohlenstoff* (carbon) and *Wasserstoff* (hydrogen). What Schmid had in mind is obviously carbon dioxide, not carbon or carbonic acid.

[64] "[E]volution ... is never achieved by means of association, but by *dissociation*; it never tends toward convergence, but toward *divergence* of efforts" (Bergson, 1907, p. 117).

[65] "[T]he elements into which a tendency splits up are far from possessing the same importance, or, above all, the same power to evolve" (ibid., p. 118). "[W]e are generally led to regard them as activities of which one is superior to the other and based upon it, whereas in reality they are not things of the same order: they have not succeeded one another, nor can we assign to them different grades" (ibid., p. 135).

which we come to explain our differences as "deux solutions divergentes, également élégantes d'un seul et même problème,"[66] as Bergson said about instinct and intellect. Perhaps we will generally find still one or the other important parallel in Bergson's work; thus, I would like, before dealing with your letter in more detail, to apply an introductory statement of Bergson (p. 148) to our problem: we have to bring all distinctions that we make into a too trenchant (*trop tranché*) form,[67] because we want to define only what is typical in thinking and feeling, whereas there is actually a thought hidden in every feeling, and feeling is permeating every thought. Or, as you once put it, feelings are pregnant with thoughts, and thoughts are pregnant with feelings. "Il sera toujours aisé de rendre ensuite les formes plus floues, de corriger ce que le dessin aurait de trop géométrique, enfin de substituer à la raideur d'un schéma la souplesse de la vie."[68]

In reading your letter I became clearly aware of the fact that in my eyes your standpoint is irrational. I find it absolutely incomprehensible how anybody could adjust to the object by way of abstraction: abstraction puts a distance between me and the object, and that is precisely why it prevents me from adapting to it.

Just as you want to purge your thinking, I want to purge my feeling of all projection, of all cold, lifeless calculation, of all that is purely intellectual and kills the feeling, and to raise it to the height of the truly vital feeling, which springs from my innermost sources and rises above all thinking, raise it to the height at which the feeling is pure and also crystal clear, and has risen above the clouds—which is as far beyond anything that is merely thought as your universal idea is beyond anything merely felt. It is not from fantasized and infantile

[66] "... *two divergent solutions, equally fitting, of one and the same problem*" (ibid., p. 143).

[67] "Let us say at the outset that the distinctions we are going to make will be too sharply drawn" (ibid., p. 136).

[68] "It will always be easy afterwards to soften the outlines and to correct what is too geometrical in the drawing—in short, to replace the rigidity of a diagram by the suppleness of life" (ibid., p. 137).

thoughts that I want to free my feeling, as you write, because often the most important and productive problems are enclosed within my fantasized and infantile thoughts. But I want to purge my feeling of all egocentric thoughts, of all thoughts that are directed *only* at self-development and self-love.

To purify the feeling, I need the object, and herein lies perhaps one of the main differences between our types: the object is an obstacle only to purifying the thinking, whereas it is absolutely essential and necessary for purifying the feeling. I maintain that every development of the feeling is possible only via and with an object, because feelings that are not directed at the object are probably only what you call a "physiological sensation." It was a struggle for me to finally realize that I cannot develop without the object. Thus I had to sacrifice an ideal of freedom, for I have to remain in a certain dependency on the object.

If I conceive those people with whom I have a closer relationship only as imagoes, as symbolic values of tendencies within myself, precisely that effect to which I owe the development and purification of the feelings will get lost: in doing so I cut them off from myself. Viewing things on the subjective plane, therefore, was no relief for me. It did do me the great service, however, of enabling me to see the imago in my feelings for other people, and insofar as another person represented a complex for me, it became possible for me to unlearn complex-related reactions. But if I carry my view of the other as no more than an imago too far, I will no longer be able to respond spontaneously and emotionally to him, and in my view it is in my feeling reactions that my greatest asset lies. In other words, I am depriving myself of the possibility of feeling me into the other when I view things on the subjective plane. I have to accept your explanation of my reactions on the subjective plane—to Herr Müller, for example—to the extent that he is an imago for me, or that my reaction is complex related. But even if I realize that what I do not like in Herr Müller corresponds to something I do not like in my own character, Herr Müller will still not have vanished from the earth for me. I am indeed married to him, because I need the object.

At a time when I still identified with you, I tried for several weeks to completely embrace your ideal: all my hatred and my love were nothing but reactions to imagoes, to tendencies within my own personality. I even accepted the phrase in your "Transformations and symbols of the libido": "Beauty does not reside in the things themselves, but in the feeling we attach to them,"[69] as a truth that was valid also for me. I thus succeeded in finding an attitude toward reality that was satisfying for the moment, but very soon I had to realize that by this one-sided attitude I deprived myself of any possibility of further development. I could no longer react spontaneously, my desire to feel myself into the other withered, I became lifeless, and I had the feeling I was violating myself.

So the reason why I find your standpoint irrational is that, when I assume it, I live irrationally myself. After I had realized this, there were moments when I discarded your standpoint as irrational even for you, and it seemed to me that from your standpoint it was no longer possible to love and to hate. But for me love means life. Goethe, who was more of a feeling person, wrote to Jakobi (10 May 1812), the purely intellectual one, when the latter sent him his book, *Von den göttlichen Dingen und ihrer Offenbarung* [*Of Divine Things and Their Revelation*],[70] that if he, Goethe, had published a similar work, there would have had to be an inscription on the back of the title page: "We get to know nothing but what we love, and the deeper and the fuller our knowledge is supposed to be, the more forceful, stronger, and livelier must be our love, even our passion."[71] I have to confess that I, too, firmly believe that even knowledge is predicated on love. Although I realize today that it is a one-sided standpoint if you can know only what you love. For the feeling person, however, love for the object

[69] "Die Schönheit liegt ja nicht in den Dingen, sondern im Gefühl, das wir den Dingen geben" (Jung, 1911/12, reprint 1991, p. 176). This sentence was deleted in the revised edition (1952) and so does not occur in *Symbols of Transformation* and in the CW.

[70] Jacobi, 1811. Friedrich Heinrich Jacobi (1743–1819), German polemicist, socialite, and literary figure.

[71] In M. Jacobi, 1846, p. 254.

does play this great role. I know that this standpoint is diametrically opposed to yours, and I can understand today that you find it as irrational as I find yours. Perhaps we could also explain the urge toward abstraction and toward feeling-into like this: the urge represents a need to be relieved and liberated. The thinking person tries, through abstraction, to liberate himself from the object, from reality, which represents chaos to him; the feeling person tries, by feeling himself into the object, to liberate himself from himself, and from his chaotic feelings. The tendency toward liberation in the thinking person leads away from the object, that of the feeling person leads toward the object.

If we, you and I, could lead a separate existence side by side, undisturbed by each other, we would now be in agreement, in that each of us tries to accept the viewpoint of the other, even if considering it irrational. The past months seem to confirm, in my view, that our mutual relationship is not realized if each of us leads his separate existence. By the fact that we enter into a relationship with each other, one of us becomes an object for the other. My natural way leads me (if I may express myself one-sidedly on purpose) to feel myself into the object, whereas yours leads you away from the object. When I imagine that I represent mostly an imago for you, an imago, that is, which for you has the symbolic value of the irrational, it seems to me that you will not be capable of responding spontaneously to me. Also, when I think that I am mostly an imago for you, I feel I am being devalued, which in turn makes it nearly impossible for me to respond spontaneously toward you. I know that in making this statement I am exaggerating in a schematic way, but I find this necessary. I can imagine that a purely intellectual person would find it quite pleasant to be viewed by others as nothing but an imago; he would thus be protected against their spontaneous feeling reactions. But for the feeling person it is impossible to feel himself into another individual for whom he represents more or less exclusively an imago, because he feels that all reactions of the other are directed not to him or to his personality but only to an imago within the other.

In my view, this seems to be one of the difficulties with which we are confronted. For my part, I see a solution in my reaching the insight that what is irrational to me may be rational to me at the same time, because I must not accept only one truth, the truth that follows from the objective plane. I must learn to see that "all that is changeable is *also* but reflected."[72] But I must not view each object that presents itself to me primarily as *only* a symbol. Perhaps the same is true for you; primarily, the object can be only an imago for you, secondarily, however, a certain feeling into the object will be necessary for you, too.[73]

Perhaps the antagonistic, yet complementary relation between the two types, as assumed above, consists in the fact that they force each other to place more emphasis on the person's own standpoint, but then also to exchange it for the other one. I'll write more about how I see this later.

With best regards,
your Hans Schmid

[72] An allusion to Goethe's *Faust* (part II): "All that is changeable is but reflected / The unattainable here is effected / Human discernment here is passed by / The Eternal-Feminine draws us on high."

[73] Crossed out: I would be interested in hearing your views on this.

3 J

[undated]

Dear Friend,

Before I respond to the particular questions raised in your letter, I would like to deal with a question of terminology.

We speak of "thinking" and "feeling," and we name the types concerned accordingly. As you know, I have introduced these types in an earlier publication, under the names of the introverted and the extraverted type.[74] For the former, adaptation proceeds via abstraction from the object, for the latter, via feeling into the object.[75] The term "introversion" thus describes an inward turning of the psychic energy, which I called "libido," because the introvert does not comprehend the object directly, but by means of abstraction, that is, by a thinking process that is inserted between himself and the object. The attitude he assumes toward the object is a certain *rejection*, therefore, which can even develop into a kind of fear of the object. His primary reaction toward the object is actually not love but rather fear.[76] The ancients knew these two original powers well, the *eros* and *phobos*.[77] It is not permissible to say that fear of the object is just a repression of an unbearable love of the object, because then we could also say that the extravert's characteristic love of the object is nothing but a repression of an unbearable fear of the object. It is more likely that in the unconscious of the introvert there is a love for the object that compensates his fear of it, while in the unconscious

[74] Jung 1913a. See the introduction for the prehistory of this pairing.

[75] Already in 1913, Jung had equated Worringer's notions of "feeling-into" and "abstraction" with his concepts of extraversion and introversion respectively (1913a, §§ 871–73). Cf. Shapiro & Alexander, 1975.

[76] "To the introverted type the universe does not appear to be beautiful and desirable, but disquieting and even dangerous" (1913a, § 873).

[77] Greek for love and fear; in the original, written in Greek letters.

of the extravert there is a fear that compensates his love for the object.[78] In pathological cases, as you know, unconscious love also becomes a source of heightened fear of the object for the introvert, and, conversely, unconscious fear becomes a source of powerful attraction to the object for the extravert.

These remarks may characterize the choice of the terms introversion and extraversion sufficiently enough, so that we will be able to use them in further discussions. We thus also avoid a possible misunderstanding, namely, that the thinking person is characterized by the absence of feeling, and the feeling person by the absence of thinking, which would certainly be completely wrong. The introvert does feel, too, and very intensely so, only in a different way than the extravert does.

Turning now to your letter, you state that you find it inconceivable that one could adapt to the object by way of abstraction. This is actually the leitmotif for all misunderstandings between extraverts and introverts. They misunderstand each other thoroughly as far as their behavior toward the object is concerned. Despite your optimism, so characteristic of the extravert, I find this difference somewhat deplorable. (This is where the feeling of the introvert comes into play.) For it is this difference that causes many of the most painful experiences in life, and many of the most acrimonious fights over attitudes and views of the world.

In my last letter, I described the introverted and the extraverted ideal to you, namely, the desire of each type to crystallize its pure essence. Now this description has already led to a kind of misunderstanding. I did not express any personal conviction with this description, nor did I want to convey an ex-

[78]This is in accordance with Jung's view that the unconscious in general has a compensatory function: "In normal people, the principal function of the unconscious is to effect a compensation and to produce a balance. All extreme conscious tendencies are softened and toned down through a counter-impulse in the unconscious" (Jung, 1914b, § 449). If this potentially salutary compensatory influence is ignored, or cannot be integrated, as in pathological developments, it will, according to Jung, lead to a still more one-sided conscious attitude in the individual, while the unconscious content will appear in a projected form and become a source of intense fascination and/or fear.

pression of my personal opinion through it, but I was thinking *hypothetically*. This hypothetical thinking—which is by no means the expression of a personal opinion—is extraordinarily misleading for the extravert, because he is always inclined to understand such an expression in a concrete way. Conversely, the introvert is always led by the nose by the extravert and by *hypothetical feeling*. I will try to describe this difficult problem in more detail on the basis of your letter but cannot guarantee that I will succeed.

You write: "To purify the feeling I need the object," and you add that for the introvert "the object is only an obstacle to purifying thinking." Herein lies a great misunderstanding. The introvert needs the object for his thinking, because it is precisely via the object that he adapts to outer reality. I'd like to say that this is exactly where his mistake lies: *He thinks objects*, instead of feeling them, for these objects are, after all, human beings who quite refuse to be only thought, although the introvert fancies that he is actually loving the object in this way. The object, however, experiences the fact of being only thought as very unpleasant, as you have rightly stated. Whereas the extravert needs the object to bring his type to perfection and to cleanse his feeling, the introvert experiences this as a horrible violation and disrespect of his personality, because he absolutely refuses to be, so to speak, the chemical dry cleaner for the feelings of extraverts. He cannot follow the other's *hypothetical feeling*, which feels like a loveless experiment to him. He feels it in this way because he feels concretistically,[79] while the extravert can *feel abstractly* beyond the object, just as the introvert can *think abstractly* beyond the object, which naturally is felt as equally loveless by the extravert. So while you resist being merely thought by me, I resist serving you as an object for the cleansing of your feelings. This contrast is irreconcilable, unless, that is, you stoop to submitting completely to my thinking, or I throw

[79] Cf. Jung, 1921, §§ 696–99, where he speaks of "concretism" as a "peculiarity of thinking and feeling which is the antithesis of abstraction," and asserts that it is a "primitivism" invariably linked to specific material or bodily sensations, which makes abstraction impossible.

myself at the feet of your feeling. This is impossible, of course, but it does happen all the time in reality, in marriages, for example, in which one part is pinioned against the wall precisely by the other's "love," not to mention those cases in which this happens through open violence. The tragedy is that it is exactly this love, which is ideal in his eyes, that violates and debases the other.

You think the introvert does not need the object for his thinking, because it would actually represent an obstacle to him, and that therefore he would not love the object. Exactly the opposite is the case. He, too, loves the object, but through his thinking; indeed, it is indispensable for his thinking. This is not so for the extravert. For him, the object is an obstacle to his thinking, because his thinking disregards the object. Here I must remind you of my previous letter, namely, of the passage where I speak of the difference between thinking and representation.[80] The representation of the extravert refers completely to the object and is, therefore, in complete agreement with *outer reality*, while his thinking is in agreement with his own *inner reality*. This is not the case in the introvert. His representation of things is inadequate, precisely because of the lack of feeling-into [the object]. His thinking is in accordance with outer reality, but not with his own inner reality. This explains the often-observed fact that the introvert thinks and preaches all sorts of nice things but does not do them himself, in fact, does the contrary; whereas the extravert does all sorts of good and nice things but does not think them, in fact, often the contrary. This also explains the social behavior of the two types. The extravert has flourishing social contacts, the introvert does not. The extravert knows, by feeling himself into others, by what human means people can be won over, whereas the introvert tries to create values in himself

[80] Cf. the end of 1 J: "[W]hat the feeling person calls thinking is just a *representation* but not an abstraction. His approach to thinking is therefore extraordinarily concretistic, and it is immediately noticeable that it cannot turn into an abstraction. Vice versa, the feeling of the thinking person is not at all what the feeling person would call feeling but is really a *sensation*, as a rule of a reactive nature, and thus very concretistic, if not to say 'physiological.'"

with which he tries to impress and force others toward him, or even bring them to his knees. He does this with the help of the *power principle*, while the extravert does it with the pleasure-unpleasure mechanism.[81] Or with [...][82] characterizes the introvert.

This formula, like all formulas, is only partly valid, that is, valid only to a certain degree. The more ideal the attitude of a type is, the more likely his plan will fail. For if I develop an ideal attitude I will become one-sided. If I am one-sided, however, I will stretch the pairs of opposites in my nature apart, thus activating the unconscious standpoint that runs directly counter to my own ideal. The introvert gives away his values in an impersonal way, becomes impoverished in the process, and finally thinks: How come you still do not want to do it? Namely, to love me? But the others have simply been put off, or been degraded to slaves, by his showing off all the time, and nobody has noticed that all he really wanted was to win the simple human love of others by this. That is also why the introvert tends to fall for some highly inferior "love."

I recently witnessed the opposite case, a famous extraverted teacher who, with truly untold love and devotion, educated her students to master their art.[83] When the girls had completed their training, however, they were on their way out and wanted to practice their art in their own way. The teacher broke down in desperation over the black ingratitude of those people who brought all her love to ruins and simply did not want to stay collaborating with her forever. Despite the purely ideal nature of all her devotion, she had completely forgotten that her tenderly loved objects were also human beings who preferred individual independence to ideal slavery. Consciously, the teacher was completely devoted to her ideal task and was

[81] Cf. Jung's earlier linking of Freud's theory ("pleasure-unpleasure") with extraversion, and Adler's ("power principle") with introversion (see Introduction).

[82] A part of the sentence is illegible here.

[83] It is possible that Jung is referring to his patient Suzanne Perrottet, the director of Rudolf von Laban's dance school in Zurich (cf. Wolfensberger, 1995).

completely *selfless*. Unconsciously, however, the opposite became more and more strained, and this opposite was her *unconscious power principle*. Conversely, the introvert strains the pleasure-unpleasure mechanism in his unconscious by the conscious, idealistic desire to create the highest values proper to force others to come to him, thus degrading people to objects of his desire.

Thus, it comes that the extravert, with his idealistic attitude, gathers inferior followers around him who, although they seem to be faithfully and gratefully devoted to him, actually flatter his unconscious power principle in Byzantine ways. Independent persons turn away from him, however—ungratefully, as he says—which naturally makes him feel misunderstood in his most ideal values.

The ideally[84] oriented introverted person is faced with the fact that he scares away from himself precisely the human love and joy that he is really trying to find behind all his desire to impress and to be superior, and that he keeps and chains to himself only those inferior persons who know best how to cater to his desire. This explains, for instance, the well-known fixation of introverted scholars or other intellectually superior persons to women of an inferior type, to whores and the like. The fault lies in straining the ideal, typical attitude too much.

Now the solution of this problem is intimately connected with what I call the *interpretation on the subjective plane*. The only goal for the ideally oriented introvert is the *production of impersonal, imperative values*, and for the equally ideally oriented extravert the only goal is the *love for the object. But both these endeavors are of a hypothetical nature.* They do not express man's true nature but are only hypotheses about how the desired goal might be reached. While the introvert's conscious attitude is an impersonal and just attitude of power, his unconscious attitude aims at inferior lust and pleasure; and while the extravert's conscious attitude is a personal love

[84] "Ideal" here used in a philosophical sense, as in the concept of a "pure" or "ideal" type, not in a moral or judgemental sense. Cf. the discussion of the "ideally oriented type" and of "ideal striving" in the introvert and extravert in this and the following letters.

for human beings, his unconscious attitude aims at unjust, tyrannical power.

The interpretation on the subjective plane is trying to mediate between the two. *Its aim is to help the individual accept his unconscious opposite*, and not, as you think, to reinterpret the other as *nothing but* a symbol, so as to protect him from affective influence. This would be a prejudice. The formula on the subjective plane for both types runs rather as follows:

Introversion: I have to realize that my object, apart from its reality, is *also* a symbol of my pleasure, which I unconsciously try to gratify with its help.[85]

Extraversion: I have to realize that my object, apart from its reality, is *also* a symbol of my power, the approval of which I try to obtain from it.

This interpretation on the subjective plane will not, in my view, prevent spontaneous reactions but leads only to a higher degree of self-reflection, and thus liberates us from the confusing projections of unconscious wishes, which violate the object and thereby prevent the conscious, ideal striving from being completely successful.

To deal in more detail with a few more points, I would like to draw your attention to the passage in your letter where you refer to my phrase: "Beauty does not reside in the things themselves, but in the feeling we attach to them." In general terms, this statement is true. A short reference to the universal confusion about the notion of beauty suffices to prove the subjectivity of aesthetic judgements. For instance, it is not only exotic music that sounds abominable to our ears, but there is even music and other pieces of art in our own culture that some people praise as beautiful, while others turn away with aching ears and eyes. Your feeling of being violated, which the acceptance of this statement brought about in you, is due not to its general correctness but to the fact that you simply accepted it

[85] In *Liber Novus*, Jung discussed the dynamic interrelation between forethinking or thought (represented in his fantasies by Elijah) and pleasure (represented by Salome). He wrote: "May the thinking person accept his pleasure, and the feeling person accept his own thought" (2009, p. 294).

from me. By this you violated your own thinking. The same thing will happen to the introvert if he simply accepts the other's love without having made a personal effort to win it.

Furthermore, I take exception to your partially true statement that "the thinking person tries, through abstraction, to liberate himself from the object, from reality, which represents chaos to him."

I would say: the introvert also tries, through the hypothesis of abstraction, to reach the object, actually reality, which seems to him chaotic only because of the projection of his unused and therefore undeveloped feeling. He tries to conquer the object by thinking. But he wants to reach the object quite as much as the extravert. The extravert does want to get to the object but actually only to come to himself by going beyond the object. He has fled from himself, because his unused and, therefore, chaotic world of thoughts has made it unpleasant, even unendurable, for him to stay with himself.

In order to develop their distinctive features both types need to exist separately to a certain extent; and if they realize their own respective unconscious opposite, they will complement each other beautifully. But, because of the nonacceptance of the unconscious opposite, the typical ideal striving leads to a disastrous violation of the other, and the worst thing is that neither of them notices why he is violating the other. I believe we are experiencing something of this kind at present, in the conflict between the Roman and the Germanic cultural ideals, which can be felt also in Switzerland.

With best regards,
your Jung

4 S

6. VII. 15

Dear Friend,

I did not take your remarks in the first letter as an expression of your personal statement. I contrasted your hypothetical thinking with my hypothetical feeling in hypothesizing that your remarks were your personal conviction. I reacted to this hypothesis, but I was well aware of the fact that it was only a hypothesis. I find it absolutely mandatory that we should give each other the credit to assume that neither of us wants to react in a personal way against the other; but we must, in order to get spontaneous reactions, adopt the attitude that each of us writes *as if* the one would think in this way, and the other feel in this way.

In order to avoid further misunderstandings, which I believe are looming, I would like, before going into your letter in more detail, to communicate the following views to you. In your first letter you write of two kinds of truth, and you will probably remember that I told you months ago that in my view everybody had to solve two mutually opposed problems. In accordance with my type, I have since called these problems "ideals." Now I think that what you mean by two kinds of truth, and what I call two ideals, to be identical, but that this duality is actually not identical with the two types, although it seems to be so from the standpoint of each individual. Allow me, the concrete or objective [*gegenständlich*] (as Goethe calls it)[86] or symbolic thinker, to make myself clear with the help of an image.

[86]The German psychiatrist and philosopher Johann Christian August Heinroth (1773–1843) characterized Goethe's way of thinking as "concrete" or "objective" [*gegenständlich*]. Goethe fully agreed with this characterization, for example, in his essay "Significant help from a single clever word," quoted by Schmid later on in this letter.

Once, on a motorboat trip, Fräulein Moltzer[87] compared the introvert to a motorboat and the extravert to a sailing boat.[88] Now let us imagine that we are going on a trip, you in the motorboat, and I in the sailing boat. Suddenly the wind drops, and I feel it as a violation when you leave in your motorboat. I insist on being taken in tow by you, which you in turn feel as a violation. On another trip you run out of gas, but I have a good wind, and we are faced with the opposite situation. As we want to stay together, and have learned from those experiences, you will now put mast and sail in your motorboat, and I a motor in my sailing boat. One can easily imagine a situation in which all his thinking no longer helps the introvert, and he has to feel, and conversely also a situation in which feeling himself into the object no longer helps the extravert, and he has to think.

Now, what I would like to call two kinds of truth or two different ideals is this: your ideal is to construct your motor in a way that a defect is as unlikely as possible, and that it uses as little gas as possible; my analogous ideal is to construct my sailing boat in a way that it can make use of the slightest puff of wind. Now this ideal is in contrast, for you as for me, with another ideal, namely, of coping with the situation by[89] another appliance, so that the sailor can make the trip even without wind by using a motor, and the one in the motorboat without motor by using a sail. I would like to call the first ideal that of *deepening one's own personality*, and the second one that of *adaptation to reality*.

These two truths probably run parallel to the two truths that Pastor Keller[90] once derived for us from the gospels; the

[87] Maria Moltzer (1874–1944), daughter of the owner of the Dutch liquor factory Bols, became a nurse in protest against the misuse of alcohol. She was trained by Jung as a psychotherapist, became a member of his closer circle, and from 1913 on worked as an analyst in Zurich. Cf. Shamdasani, 1998b, pp. 103–6.

[88] Here some lines inserted in the margin are heavily crossed out.

[89] Crossed out: heterogeneous.

[90] Adolf Keller (1872–1963), Swiss pastor and theologian, a member of the circle around Jung, later an active member of the Psychological Club. Cf. Jehle-Wildberger, 2009, and his wife's description of him in her memoirs (Swann, 2011).

one puts the value of the individual soul above everything, the other the value of the realm of God. I do not think, however, that these two coincide with the various problems of the two types, for both types carry both ideals within themselves. Those ideals run directly counter to each other, because in both types the tendency to develop one's personality prevents adaptation, and adaptation itself prevents the deepening of one's personality. So each of the types believes that the *other* truth[91] is the problem of the other type; this other truth only implies, however, that he himself should also solve the problem of the other, while it is not the other's problem as such. What I called the ideal of deepening one's own personality you call, in your last letter, the "typical ideal striving," and the man who strives for it, "the ideally oriented." Striving for adaptation to reality would then correspond to what you write in your first letter: "[M]an, ever mindful of his role as homo sapiens, tries to tame and control the irrational with the rational," or to what you call, in your last letter, "the acceptance of the unconscious opposite." You admit that typical ideal striving is one-sided, but it seems to me that in that one-sidedness there also lies what is important, valuable, and at the same time dangerous.

Nature always follows the principle of economy, so that one partner should not concern himself exclusively with perfecting his motor, while not using the good winds, or that the other should not only let himself be driven by the wind and stand still when the wind drops. Therefore, I would like to call, from my point of view, the one-sided striving for the perfection of one's personality the irrational truth, and the striving for utilizing one's faculties for adaptation to reality as much as possible the rational truth. I believe that there is a great danger in striving for the latter, namely, of becoming shallow, precisely because it runs counter to the tendency of deepening one's personality. A motorboat made into half a sailing boat will lose its value, and vice versa. I can also imagine very well that a perfect sailor, who has developed his capacity for feeling-into to the highest degree, believes that he does not need the

[91] Crossed out: which seems irrational to him.

motor or thinking; and, conversely, that an expert with the motorboat, an intellectually superior person, has so much confidence in his gas supply and in the reliability of his motors that he does not want to be bothered by sailing or feeling. But you yourself say: "The more ideal the attitude of a type is, the more likely his plan will fail." Both tendencies applied exclusively, therefore, harbor dangers, and yet both are beneficial, even necessary. And thus it perhaps boils down, once again, to the old maxim: "Do the one thing while not neglecting the other."

If I now try to apply these views to your letter, what I call adaptation to reality is what you call "accordance with outer reality," and the deepening of one's one personality, "accordance with inner reality." It is not from the fact that there are two types that the two kinds of truth are derived, in my view, but from the fact that for each of the two types there exist two kinds of reality, an inner and an outer one. Certainly the attitudes toward these realities, ideals, or truths taken by each of the two types are very different. I believe the introvert tries above all to develop his personality and to make inner reality harmonious, and he hopes to be able to adapt to reality in this way. The extravert, on the other hand, tries above all to adapt to outer reality, and hopes in this way to develop his personality. This may be the reason why the extravert is driven by something outside himself (by the wind, by feeling that depends on the object). He soon notices, however, that this one-sided attitude does not satisfy him. The introvert, on the other hand, has the force that causes movement (the motor) in himself, and is, *eo ipso*,[92] less dependent on reality. Perhaps we can also put it like this: the conscious striving of the introvert aims at the development of his personality, at the creation of impersonal values, as you call it, and only the acknowledgement of the unconscious opposite leads him to an adaptation to reality. The conscious striving of the extravert, on the other hand, aims at adaptation to reality, and only acknowledging his unconscious opposite will lead him to develop his own personality. The interpretation on the subjective plane leads both of

[92] Latin for "by that very act (or fact)."

them to acknowledge the unconscious opposite and is, therefore, of the greatest importance for the extravert, too. I do not believe that the liberation of the extravert is possible through the interpretation on the subjective plane, however, because this interpretation leads him away from adaptation to reality. In my view, as I shall elaborate later, real liberation will be possible only if the ideal of adaptation to reality is *also* striven for.

It was very interesting for me to find that Goethe, that extraverted man, repeatedly expressed mistrust of carrying self-knowledge and the development of one's personality too far, a mistrust I also felt in recent years toward certain trends in analysis. Thus, in a short essay, "Significant help from a single clever word,"[93] Goethe wrote: "Here I confess that the great and so high-sounding task, 'Know thyself!' has always appeared suspect to me, the ploy of secretly allied priests who wanted to confuse man by making unattainable demands on him, and to lead him away from activity directed at the outer world toward false inner tranquillity. Man knows himself only so far as he knows the world, of which he becomes aware only in himself, and of himself only in it." In a similar vein he wrote to Fr[iedrich von] Müller on 8 March 1824: "I maintain that man can never get to know himself, can never observe himself purely as an object. Others know me better than I know myself. I can only know and correctly assess my relations to the outer world, and this is what we should confine ourselves to. With all the striving for self-knowledge, of which priests and morals preach to us, we do not advance in life, and achieve neither results nor true inner improvement."[94] (Cf. also Goethe to Eckermann, 10 April 1829.)[95]

[93] "Bedeutende Fördernis durch ein einziges geistreiches Wort" (1823).

[94] Burkhardt, 1870, p. 1939. Friedrich von Müller (1779–1849) was chancellor of the grand duchy of Sachsen-Weimar-Eisenach and a close friend of Goethe (cf. ibid., *Einleitung*).

[95] There Goethe said: "Throughout the ages people have said again and again that one should try to know oneself. This is a strange demand with which nobody has complied so far, and with which actually nobody should comply. With all his thoughts and wishes man is dependent upon the external, upon the world around him, and he is occupied enough with knowing it and making use of it to the extent that he needs it for his purposes. He knows of

Goethe's standpoint may be one-sided, but nevertheless it seems to me of value as a counterbalance to an overemphasis on the tendency to self-development.

Now, your letter has taught me that in my last letter I made a mistake in the form of a projection. Because my abstract thinking leads away from the object, I believed that yours did, too. But I have the impression that you have a similarly wrong view of the extravert, or I will at least assume it hypothetically. Your example of the teacher does not fit with how I see the extravert. If that teacher had really been selfless, and had really felt herself into her students, she would have felt and understood their drive for independence, and her very love would have forced her to honor it. The teacher's reactions are in my opinion those of a selfish mother, not those typical of an extravert. She reacted in the way she did not because she was extraverted but because she wanted to be a mother.

From the fact that you chose this example, I venture to conclude that you believe the extravert does not consider the object in his abstract feeling (in his love), just as I believed the introvert did not consider the object in his abstract thinking. I would now like to apply one phrase in your letter to the extravert, in the following way:[96] you think the extravert does not consider the object in his abstract feeling because it is an outright obstacle for him (owing to an unconscious power tendency, as you suppose), and that when he feels abstractly and selflessly, therefore, he does not really love the object at all.[97] Exactly the opposite is the case. He loves the object through his feeling; indeed, it is indispensable for his feeling.

This is not so in the introvert. For him the object is an obstacle to his feeling, because his feeling disregards the object. But apart from this feeling, which disregards the object, the

himself only when he enjoys or suffers, and thus he is taught about himself, and what he has to seek and to avoid, only by suffering or joy. But man is a dark being, by the way, and he does not know from where he comes nor where he goes, he knows little of the world, and least about himself. I do not know myself either, and God beware I should" (Eckermann, 1835, p. 376).

[96] Regarding the following sentence, Jung noted in the margin: nonsense.

[97] The following two sentences inserted in the margin.

introvert also has sensation, which is as closely related to the object as is the representation of the extravert. You even said it was of a reactive nature. This sensation is in complete accordance with outer reality, while the feeling of the introvert is in accordance with his inner reality. This is not so in the extravert. His sensation of things is inadequate because of his lack of thinking. His feeling is in accordance with outer reality but not with his own inner reality. If the teacher's feeling had been in accord with outer reality, she would have loved her students selflessly and honored their independence.[98] She was not able to do this, because she still had an archaic attitude toward them. The feeling of the extravert is not influenced by the unconscious power principle, precisely because it is not in accordance with his inner reality, just as the abstract thinking[99] of the introvert is not influenced by the unconscious search for pleasure.

To make myself even clearer, I would like to use a graphical schema, although I can imagine that you as an introvert will have little sympathy for it. Outer reality is the same for both types, only their adaptation to it is different; inner reality is different for each of them, however. Guided by this idea I arrive at the following schema:[100]

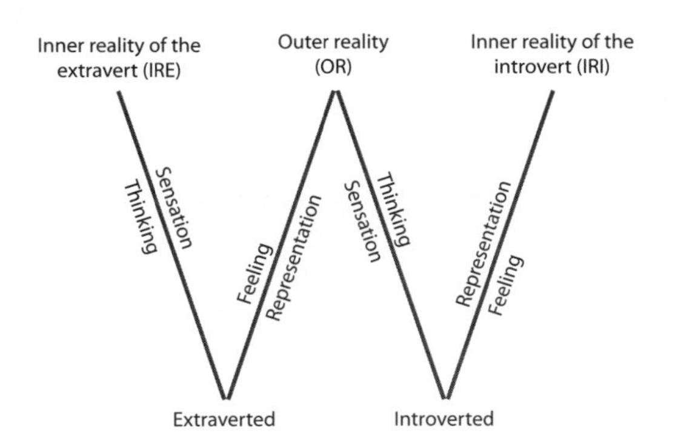

[98] This sentence added in the margin.
[99] Corrected from: feeling.
[100] Cf. Jung's later fourfold diagram of the functions (Jung, 2012, p. 128).

I now realize that in my last letter I wrongly assumed that, since my tendency E[xtravert]-IRE is in accordance with inner reality, it would be the same for your corresponding tendency I[ntrovert]-OR. This was where I made a projection. I ask myself, however, if the introvert is not also inclined to assume that the tendency E-OR of the extravert leads as much to inner reality as his own corresponding tendency I-IRI. Since my thinking and sensation are in accordance with my inner reality, or let us say for short, *egocentric*, I assumed that yours were, too; and since your representation and feeling are in accordance with your inner reality, thus equally egocentric, you probably also found it suggestive to assume the same for me. In other words, we thought the tendencies E-IRE and I-OR on the one hand, and E-OR and I-IRI on the other, were identical, and this resulted in the feeling that the one did not do justice to the other, that the one was violating the other.

As far as this feeling of being violated is concerned, I naturally expected you to resist serving as an object for purifying my feelings, just as I resisted being merely thought. There is nothing irreconcilable in this difference for me, however. As a matter of fact, I have never felt this opposite nature of the two types as anything tragic but only saw a meaningful interaction of nature in it. What you felt as a violation, I felt as a meaningful force. I felt this force as unpleasant, or as a violation, only so long as I believed I had to submit completely to your thinking, to let my sailing boat be towed by your motorboat. The more I developed my abstract thinking, putting a motor in my sailing boat, the more I felt this force as salutary. It forced me to perfect my motor more and more. So I need not submit to your thinking but to my own, although I know that my motor will not be as perfect as yours for the time being. At the end of your letter you write yourself that I feel violated only so long as I violate my own thinking (instead of submitting myself to it). Vice versa, it seems to me that the introvert will feel the love of the extravert as a violation only so long as he believes he has to throw himself at the feet of the feeling of the extravert, to let himself be towed by the extravert's sailing boat, or, as you put it, so long as he simply accepts the love of the other.

The more the introvert learns to use his motorboat also as a sailing boat, the more he no longer violates his own feelings but tries to develop them instead (even if they are less sophisticated than those of the extravert), and the less he will experience the love of the extravert as a violation but more as a salutary force. Or, in short, the opposites are irreconcilable only so long as the extravert—because he himself cannot think—does not feel accepted by the introvert, and the introvert—because he himself cannot love—feels violated by the love of the extravert.

Now one could imagine that an arrangement between the two types could be found, in which the extravert accepts the introvert's striving for the creation of impersonal values as an expression of love, and the introvert the love of the extravert as the latter's impersonal value. In that way each would encourage the other in his one-sided ideal striving. But I do not think that this corresponds with our nature. The introvert who tries out this solution would probably soon ask himself, What use is the extravert's love to me if he has no real impersonal values? And the extravert would ask himself, What use are the impersonal values of the introvert to me if he cannot give them to me with love? Therefore, I would like to expand your formulas for the two types as follows:

Introversion: I have to realize that my object, apart from its reality, is *not only* the symbol of my inferior *pleasure* to me, which I seek to gratify through it, but also the object of a higher conscious *love*, which I have to develop out of the unconscious, inferior pleasure in the object.

Extraversion: I have to realize that my object, apart from its reality, is *not only* the symbol of my unjust, tyrannical *power* to me, the approval of which I seek to get from it, but also an object through which I have to develop the conscious *strength* of my personality out of the unconscious, tyrannical striving for power.

In other words, the introvert not only must wish to develop himself in order to be loved but also must love in an active way in order to develop. The extravert not only must love in order to develop but also must have the wish to develop in order to be loved. For the time being, I would just like to show how I envisage the development toward this ideal state with the help of the image we used: the more the pilot of the motorboat perfects his motor, the more his boat will rise in the water and the more he will fly across it. Eventually his motor will become so perfect that he will exchange the resistance of water for that of the air and will fly on the water. And when he then also uses the sails as wings, he will rise above the water and actually fly. The sailor, on the other hand, will gradually perfect his yachtsmanship so that he will glide more and more swiftly over the water, and gradually he will learn to use his sails as wings. When he then also uses the motor, he will be able to rise out of the water into the air. Each perfects his own characteristics at first: the one makes a propeller out of his propelling screw, the other wings out of his sails. Then he reaches a point when he can develop further only if he accepts and takes over from the other the very thing by which he felt most violated at first, the sailor the motor, and the motorboat pilot the sails.

To conclude, a word on the subjectivity of the notion of beauty. It is part of the ideal striving of the extravert that he assumes not only a subjective notion of beauty but one that lies outside him, although it can be understood only metaphysically, a concept of absolute beauty, as Plato describes it in the *Symposium*.[101] It is part of the ideal striving of the introvert that he assumes not only a subjective concept of truth but one that lies outside him, although it can be understood only metaphysically, the concept of absolute truth, or of the universally valid concept, as you called it. Going by motorboat is the search for absolute truth, sailing the search for absolute beauty. The universal confusion over the concept of beauty is as little a proof of the nonexistence of a metaphysical, absolute concept of beauty, as the equally great and universal confusion over the concept of truth is of the nonexistence of a

[101] Schmid may rather have thought of Plato's *Phaedo*, however, in which Plato discusses the general essence of qualities in general, and "absolute beauty" in particular (the so-called problem of universals).

metaphysical absolute truth. In his ideal striving the extravert needs the concept of absolute beauty, yet in order to adapt to reality he has to realize that the beauty does not lie in reality but in the feeling that he attaches to things. The introvert, in his ideal striving, cannot accept the concept of absolute beauty; he knows that the beauty lies only in his feeling. In order to adapt he has to assume, however, that the thing in itself can be beautiful and that an absolute beauty exists beyond his feeling.

In his ideal striving the introvert needs the concept of absolute truth, yet in order to adapt to reality he has to see that the truth is realized only in his thinking, not in reality. The extravert, in his ideal striving, cannot accept the concept of absolute truth; he knows that it exists only in his thinking. In order to adapt he has to assume, however, that there is a truth in itself, and that there is an absolute truth beyond his thinking. I once put the ideal in the following words: the introvert must strive for beautiful truth, and the extravert for true beauty.

Many other things could be derived from this, but for now only the following: Plato shows that only he who is driven by *eros* knows absolute beauty. Absolute truth, then, is probably known only by someone who is driven by *phobos*.

With best regards,
your Hans Schmid

5 J

[undated][102]

Dear Friend,

I would like to say in advance that in general I agree[103] with the views expressed in your letter. They are very clear and show the way that leads beyond the incongruity of the two types. Here too, as always, I have to admire the extravert's capacity to move ahead of the difficulty, and beyond it, with his feeling. The extravert feels prospectively, the introvert retrospectively, so that the latter remains longer under the impression of the difficulty.[104]

It seems to me that we are proceeding from different levels. I realized this when I read your interpretation of my example of the teacher. When I speak of the "ideally oriented" extravert, I speak of someone who is in greatest accordance with his type. This implies that such a person realizes his feeling[105] to the greatest extent, and his self-knowledge to the least extent. For this reason I would like to call precisely that teacher an ideally oriented type. She naturally makes the mistake, as can be expected, of not realizing her archaic motherly attitude because of her lack of self-knowledge. She could do this if she ever reached the subjective plane, and asked herself: "Why am I always fussing with my students? Couldn't the mistake lie with me?" Naturally she is fully justified in fussing with the object, according to her type, but

[102] The date of 7 August 1915 has been added in different handwriting within square brackets on the original.

[103] Corrected from: that I absolutely agree.

[104] Crossed out: So when I stay with the difficulty for the moment, this is not in order to diminish the value of your remarks, but to stay true to my type for another few moments.

[105] That is, his feeling for the other person (or outer "object"). At this stage of type theory, Jung had not yet formulated "introverted feeling," in which he later saw a possible form of self-knowledge.

only until the undesirable consequences appear, which are actually inevitable. If she then still persists in manipulating the object, however, she will violate it. You write that if she really loved her students she would have felt herself correctly into their psychology. Certainly, but true love presupposes self-awareness. Or do you believe that, proceeding from her unconscious motherly attitude, she could all of a sudden attain real love, without the mediation of self-knowledge? This would run counter to all experience, and would, moreover, render superfluous an analysis, which is indispensable in such a case. We know well enough that objects are needlessly tormented by such an attitude, and that, unless the objects react most vigorously, no insight at all will result. Even if the objects put up a desperate resistance, the ideally oriented person may long go on seeking the mistake outside, instead of within himself. I maintain that in this case in particular it is absolutely necessary to view this on the subjective plane, and I dispute the possibility that "real" love can be attained without the mediation of self-knowledge.[106]

Once again I must emphasize that it is not the aim of directing the understanding on the subjective plane to explain the object merely as a symbol, but to explain it *also* as a symbol. So in my view an "ideally oriented type" is not an analyzed type at all, but an unanalyzed one, someone, for example, who only has a very good sailing boat, but without a built-in motor, thus a vehicle that does not move for hours when there is no wind.

The wind comes from the outside; psychologically speaking, it comes from the object, or rather from the extravert's relation to the object. His ideal, unanalyzed attitude has the unpleasant quality, however, of expecting the other to generate the wind with which he wants to sail. This intolerable demand will lead to catastrophes if both types insist on the right of their existence. And it is not possible for only one of

[106] As Jung was to put it in *Psychological Types*: "Interpretation of an unconscious product on the subjective level reveals the presence of subjective judgments and tendencies of which the object is made the vehicle" (1921, § 813).

them to give in insofar as he will then simply fall prey to the other.[107]

I must make a few remarks concerning your interpretation of the "two truths," because I do not altogether agree with you. It seems to me that the "ideals" of both types are merely special examples of their "truth" and not just another expression for "truth." According to your approach, you call "rational truth" the use of all capacities for adaptation to reality, and "irrational truth" the one-sided striving for perfecting the personality (*nota bene*, in the way the type understands it). It is certainly *reasonable* to make use of all capacities in the fight for adaptation, and it is certainly *unreasonable* to go after a one-sided ideal—but this has nothing to do with rational or irrational truth. If one followed your argument, one-sided striving would have to be ruled out, insofar as it is unreasonable, in favor of rational striving. The only thing gained would be the very problem people suffer from, namely, a one-sided rational ideal. This is the reason why I cannot accept your view; because for me it is essential that both, the rational as well as the irrational,[108] are accepted. The two truths have indeed something to do with the two "realities," which we might call the "psychological" and the "real" one.

Both types share the error of believing that they will find their driving force in the outside world. This is the error not only of the extravert but also of the introvert. The latter is completely extraverted in his thinking, just as the extravert is in his feeling, only the introvert takes possession of the *idea* of the object, whereas the extravert takes possession of the ob-

[107] Crossed out: Therefore the introvert insists on his demand that the extravert should either wait for the wind to blow or conjure it up himself, if he is so keen on sailing. By this he forces the extravert to gain knowledge, or to think himself. The extravert should indeed insist on his demand, thus forcing the other [sentence not completed]

[108] A similar insistence on the importance of making room for the "irrational" may be found in the question Jung directed to himself after an active imagination in 1914, in which his soul had offered him the "gifts" of war, magic, and religion: "Would you really like to force everything which you are not under the yoke of your wretched knowledge and understanding?" (Jung, 2009, p. 306).

ject itself. In short, the introvert thinks with the object, the extravert feels with it. In doing so, they are both completely rational.[109] They can find their own irrational (i.e., psychological) truth only in themselves, and with it the true source of energy, because life flows from ourselves and not from the objects.

We are blinded in this respect by the spirit of our age. Not only nations but also individuals are alienated from themselves in modernity by interindividual and international relations, and they find the object of their desire always where there is already someone else. This has led to the boundless international superficiality, which is nothing but a mass phenomenon of interindividual normalization and equalization. And the latter phenomenon itself is nothing but the outflow of an archaic *collectivity* that still sticks to people. This collectivity seduces us into the erroneous belief that the other will take the same delight in being used as I do in using him.[110] This naive assumption, which is rooted in collectivity, necessarily leads to mutual fleecing and violating. Although this a priori identity with the object results in an increased adaptation to outer reality, even to the point that we can speak of a worldwide cultural thought, there is no real advantage in this, neither for a nation nor for the individual, because they both get equalized and lose their intrinsic values. The leveling-out of all

[109]This is perhaps the first time Jung explicitly speaks of thinking and feeling as both essentially "rational" functions (see note 52). His use of "rational" and "irrational" here is still different, however, from his later definition in *Psychological Types*, where he will specify that by "rational" he means "directed" functions, insofar as they "are concerned with a rational choice of objects," whereas the irrational functions of sensation and intuition "will react to every possible occurrence and be attuned to the absolutely contingent, and must therefore lack all rational direction" (Jung, 1921, § 776).

[110]Although this echoes the opening of his *Red Book* (Jung, 2009, p. 229), Jung repeatedly pointed out the danger of identifying with the collective psyche—for example, in a talk given a few months later in the "Zurich School of Analytical Psychology," in which he stated that someone doing so "will infallibly try to force the demands of his unconscious upon others, for identity with the collective psyche always brings with it a feeling of universal validity—'godlikeness'—which completely ignores all differences in the psychology of his fellows" (Jung, 1916a, § 460).

external opposites produces big newspapers, excellent railway timetables, fast connections by steamship, internationally accepted rules of conduct, like-minded convictions, international industrial and commercial organizations, and a division of labor that is carried to the extreme.

But all of this makes man, who is not a machine but many-sided, sick. *The opposites should be evened out in the individual himself.* True, this will not lead to a general "standard,"[111] to a universal ideal of the arts, the sciences, or of production of all kinds; what will emerge is what is generally not accepted, but individually valuable, what is internationally regarded as quaint or funny, but is nationally valued and alive. For man is not only a herd animal obeying a universal rule but also a "strange"[112] being. It is not only the rational truth of the herd that is vital to him but above all his irrational strangeness, the vital value of which is denied by any outsider, but which is perfectly and immediately evident to the individual; after all, this is what is his very own and his inner vitality! It is not the sameness of nations and individuals but their extreme diversity and singularity that are valuable and beautiful in them. With the spirit of international modernity, which is rooted in precisely those vestiges of archaic collectivity, we shall experience the building of a second tower of Babel, which as we know ends in a confusion of tongues. In this way nature helps herself, so that everybody will arrive at what is his own, and though it may be incomprehensible to the other, it still has the greatest vital value. This is, in my view, the irrational truth.

Just as little as I think that irrational or psychological truth is the only possible and desirable one, do I think that the development of subjectivity ("subjective plane") alone leads to the desired goal. I see adaptation to reality in the same way as Fr. Th. Vischer views morality, that is, that morality is self-evident.[113] Since such adaptation is an endless problem, not

[111] This word in English in the original.

[112] Original: *"absonderliches" Wesen*, an untranslatable play on *absonderlich* = strange, bizarre; and *(sich) absondern* = to segregate, to distance oneself.

[113] Friedrich Theodor Vischer (1807–87), German philosopher, critic, and novelist; professor in Tübingen, Zurich, and Stuttgart. In 1848 member of the

constrained by any one side[114]—for "reality" can be expanded interminably—we need some sort of standard, and this standard can never be provided by the object but only by the subject. Although the object can constrain us outwardly, it cannot do the thinking process, which sets norms and limits for us. The moral law lies within ourselves, not in the object. I have to protect the object against too much experimenting. I must also remind you of the fact that even the Freudian way of analysis aims at a change in the subjective attitude, which is brought about by a subjective, psychological process, and not at predominantly experiencing the object and doing something with it.

Moreover, I have to confess that I cannot unconditionally subscribe to Goethe's[115] statement. We must not forget that even Goethe is not the absolute authority but a human being who, as far as his unconscious is concerned, is just as small and impotent as any other insignificant person. His simile of "the ploy of secretly allied priests" clearly indicates a certain fear of the snares of the unconscious. Someone who does not have analysis—which is, after all, a most important achievement of our time—is justified, from the beginning, in being suspicious of the unconscious. For him it is undoubtedly better to stick to the "world," because he lacks the weapons to hold out against the ensnaring powers of his own unconscious. Someone of our age, however, who possesses the tools of analysis, will know how to get to the bottom of this "ploy of secretly allied priests," and he will also be able to distinguish between "false inner tranquillity" and a serious investigation of his own soul. And you know very well, by the way, that an analytical examination on the subjective plane is anything but "tranquil"; it is, on the contrary, very discomforting.

German National Assembly in Frankfurt. Best known for his work *Ästhetik, oder Wissenschaft des Schönen* [*Aesthetics, or The Science of the Beautiful*], 6 vols. (1846–57). His maxim on morality here quoted by Jung was also "a favorite quotation of [Freud's]" (Jones, 1955, p. 416; cf. Hale, 1971, p. 189).

[114] Crossed out: in which one can perish completely.

[115] Underlined in the MS.

Moreover, what Goethe says about the ineffectiveness of self-knowledge is disproved by experience and is the expression of a subjective view that is based on an equally subjective view of the nature of self-knowledge. Goethe is speaking here of his private problem, which is not generally binding. You must not suppose, by the way, that I deny the importance, in principle, of experiencing with the help of the object; I only maintain that this is often exaggerated. Too much experiencing with the help of the object, however, is also tantamount to bringing infantile fantasies into what is concrete. Yet infantile fantasy is not suited for this, for when it is transferred into the object, it becomes the most worthless and objectionable thing, but when being kept within the subject, it becomes what is most valuable, namely, the source of anything new and of further development.

From your letter I gained the impression that our views on this point are not so very far apart. It is understandable that you are a bit more in favor of the object, and I a bit more in favor of the subject.[116]

The "development of the personality" and the "creation of impersonal values" are not identical but, as already shown by the choice of these terms, of an antithetical nature. The striving for the creation of impersonal values deprives the introvert of a considerable sum of energy in the development of his personality, so that he, just as much as the extravert, in a certain sense falls behind himself (though in the opposite way than does the extravert). We must never forget that both types always contain both mechanisms, so that they would be identical, so to speak, if not for the fact that they are completely opposed.

I do not think that the object is an outright obstacle to extraverted feeling. I don't know where you get that from. All that is certain is that the extravert's abstract feeling does not

[116] Crossed out: I have to contradict your statement that the introvert has no driving force within himself. As I already said, the introvert is as extraverted in his thinking as the extravert is in his feeling. The introvert is just as little independent of the outer world as the extravert. Both have the driving force within themselves, but this can be made conscious only by someone who thinks. We must distinguish between "stimulation" and "source of energy."

really love the object, but merely *desires* it. You prove this yourself by your statement that for the extravert the object is *indispensable for his feeling*. Calves and pigs are indispensable for satisfying our hunger, but they would challenge that we love them, for they probably feel quite roughly treated when we lovingly prepare them for a meal. Because of his deficient sensation the extravert believes that his object is naturally delighted by getting his "love," just as he himself is gratified by achieving the fulfillment of his wish. The *feeling* of the extravert *corresponds to outer reality*; calves and pigs are really there to be eaten. Thus the feeling of the teacher also corresponds to outer reality: the one uses the other, the one devours the other, by cunning and force everybody fights for his place in the sun. And if he does not do it consciously, he does it unconsciously, and then claims that this is love, and he can claim this so long as he senses and feels deficiently. His object, however, does not feel loved at all. The teacher completely ruins the situation for herself, because she senses nothing and thinks nothing, but merely "loves," and because the students are *indispensable for her feeling*. Even though she may have correctly recognized the spirit of outer reality, and of the struggle for life, in her feeling she still does not recognize the powers of the interior, the power, that is, of her students' sensation and thinking. The students are not cattle for slaughter but human beings who are also struggling for their place in the sun. So I'm saying: precisely because the feeling of the extravert does not correspond to his own inner world (where there is sensation and thinking), but to outer reality with its merciless struggle for life, he is unconsciously completely steeped in the spirit of usurpation and violation. The abstract thinking of the introvert is a parallel to this. It is so much in accordance with outer reality that unconsciously it is completely saturated with, and contingent upon, the lusting for power in the world. We only have to remind ourselves of how pretentious a posture certain philosophical systems assume! Naturally the introvert tries to keep his feeling away from his thinking, but this is exactly why, eventually, it will nonetheless find its way into his thinking, in the form of lust for power, where it will occasionally break through with overwhelming force, as in Zarathustra, for example.

As far as your schema is concerned, I have to say the following: It is in accordance with my view and correctly represents it. It is certainly true that the unanalyzed introvert naively projects his psychology, and, therefore, assumes that the other feels and thinks exactly as he does. Thus he also assumes, for instance, that the feeling and representation of the extravert lead to inner reality in the same way as they do in his, the introvert's, case. I think I have shown very clearly by my earlier comments, however, that *I* am not at all of the opinion that your feeling and representation lead to inner reality; otherwise I would not have put so much emphasis on the importance of the "subjective plane." I have thus very clearly emphasized that I am deeply convinced that your feeling and representation[117] do not lead to inner reality, as they do in my case, but merely to thinking and sensation, which in my case lead to the outer world. So I did not feel violated by you at all; all I said was that the extravert violates his object.

It is altogether characteristic of the extravert that he never experiences the conflict in question as irreconcilable, or even tragic, for the simple reason that he does not think and sense the object sufficiently enough.[118] He forces the object to fight against that "love" as violently as this "love" is violent itself, because unconsciously he tyrannically takes possession of the object and can neither sense nor think how the object inwardly resists this. A strong and healthy man, who can put up with tastelessness and brutality, and who would rather kill the other than let himself be killed, will enter into this fight to the advantage of both sides. A sensitive and aesthetic man, who cannot

[117] Jung appears to be using representation or imagination (*Vorstellung*, which implies a mental picture) as a synonym for what he came to call the intuitive function in his mature typology.

[118] The formulation is equally unusual in the MS: *daß er das Object nicht genügend denkt*. There is the glimmer of a four-function model here, with feeling and intuition seen as the predominant functions in the extravert, and thinking and sensation as the predominant functions in the introvert. See the introduction for the evolution of Jung's typology.

put up with brutality, will not enter into this fight, to his and his partner's detriment. And that is tragic.[119] That is why I speak of the possibility of a tragic misunderstanding. On the other hand, we must admire how well nature has arranged this, too. The extravert forces the introvert, through the blindness of his love, to summon in self-defense all the violence and brutality from the depths of his soul, which the latter so desperately needs in his struggle for life. The energetic resistance of the introvert forces the extravert, in turn, to realize all the shortcomings of his thinking and sensation, which had hampered him in the fight for adaptation in that they prevented him from intellectually grasping the situation adequately.

It is certainly true, as you say, that the opposites between the introvert and the extravert are irreconcilable only so long as the two types have not reached a compensation through their unconscious opposite, just as the opposites between the summit of Montblanc and sea level are irreconcilable only so long as Montblanc is not lowered by more than 2,000 meters, and the sea level raised by more than 2,000 meters.[120] A very simple procedure in theory, but somewhat more difficult in practice! Practically speaking, compensation by the unconscious opposite turns out to be a cardinal question, which not only causes us to rack our brains but also breaks our hearts. So there is every guarantee that the procedure of leveling and evening out is, if not a hopeless, then at least an extremely difficult task.

The introvert has a reactive type of loving, but an active type of thinking. The extravert has a reactive type of thinking, but an active type of loving. A person's energy is always revealed by his activity. That is his light; his shadow[121] lies in his

[119] The following sentence was added in the margin, instead of this crossed-out sentence: Of course, there is nothing tragic for someone who does not see the tragedy.

[120] The Montblanc on the Swiss-Italian border is the highest mountain in Europe and 4,810 meters (15,780 feet) high.

[121] Already in his early work, Jung had quite frequently used the shadow metaphor in various contexts—for example, with reference to "a sleep- or dream-state" (1902, § 74), to Binet's expression of "the psychic shadow side" (1903, § 340), to the "shadowy existence" of complexes" (1913b, § 306), or to

reactions. So according to the tenor of your last letter, the goal toward which we are moving would promise nothing less than that the shadow will turn into light. With regard to physics, however, we also have to consider our energy balance and its requirements. Is human energy really strong enough, besides maintaining the light it has already created, to turn the shadow into light? I fear we might be on the road to godlikeness,[122] or at least about to create that completely spherical Platonic primordial being, whom, as we know, a god found it necessary to divide into two.[123] If we continue to pursue this road, namely, of compensating ourselves by our own unconscious opposite, we will arrive at fatal mythological analogies, one of which I have already mentioned. For if we succeeded in activating even our shadow, and thereby bring about an all-sided or two-sided activity in ourselves, the shadow of the god would threaten to cut us in two, as it did with Plato's orbicular and perfectly equipped primordial being. As you know, this Platonic myth is a later echo of the earlier, widespread original idea of the first pair of parents, who were pressed together, lying on top of each other for aeons, all-round and positive, until one day a son arose between them, who, to their surprise, separated them. Just as light and shadow always follow one another, positive and negative electricity always attract each other. Two positive charges repel each other, however. Thus we, too, might find that our activated, luminous shadow will

---

Kant's "shadowy representations" (1914b, § 440). In 1912 he had defined the "shadow-side of the psyche" as our "unrecognized desires, which, when conscious, come into violent conflict with our moral convictions" (Jung, 1912, § 438). The use of this metaphor here "foreshadows" Jung's later concept of the "shadow" as the "'negative' part of the personality, i.e., the sum of the hidden and unfavorable qualities, of the insufficiently developed functions, and the contents of the personal unconscious" (Jung, 1943, § 103[5]; trans. mod.).

[122] Cf. note 110, and Jung's remarks on (Adler's concept of) "godlikeness" in 1916a, §§ 453ff.

[123] In Plato's *Symposium*, 190–91, Aristophanes says that at the beginning all humans were spherical beings, each with four legs, four arms, two heads facing in opposite directions, and two sets of genitals. The gods then decided to cut each being in half. Since then human beings have been looking for their lost half (Plato, 1961, pp. 542–43).

suddenly separate itself from our actual light, as if it were repelled by an invisible power that interposes itself between the two centers of activity like a new shadow.

Naturally, this possibility arises only if we assume that it is at all possible to activate the shadow as well. I certainly have to concede that all kinds of things are possible in humans, of which no one has dreamt in heaven and earth.[124] We have seen people making virtues out of their vices and, as Nietzsche says, a god out of their seven devils.[125] So why shouldn't it be possible to raise the merely reactive side in our nature to activity? It is actually more a question of time, and of goodwill and faith, than a question of whether this is possible at all. We are bound, however, to our energy balance. The energy we need to activate the shadow must necessarily be withdrawn from somewhere else. And it can be withdrawn only from a place where energy can be found, that is, from thinking for the introvert, and from feeling for the extravert. Through the withdrawal of energy, the active qualities are reduced to the level of a certain dullness. Instead of a bright light and a dark shadow, there will be twilight everywhere. We believe we can see something of the sort in certain oriental psychologies of religion, in which it is precisely the recognition of the shadow that led to the harmonization and leveling-out of the psychological opposites. The legend of the life of Buddha bears testimony to this. And what insights in this respect do we not owe to the superior mind of Lao Tzu!

But I will not further deal with this problem at this point, in order to hear your opinion.[126]

[124] "There are more things in heaven and earth, Horatio, / Than are dreamt of in your philosophy" (Shakespeare, *Hamlet*, act I, scene 5).

[125] "Solitary man, *you are going the way to yourself! And your way leads past yourself* and your seven devils!" (Nietzsche, 1885, section 1, "The way of the creator," p. 90; passage as underlined in Jung's German copy). With thanks to Sonu Shamdasani.

[126] Crossed out: As far as your final passage about the metaphysical concepts of beauty and truth is concerned, I have to say that you come close to Plato with this, just as in your remarks on the compensation of the types. Ideally speaking, it [sentence not completed]

To conclude, I would like to come back to the "metaphysical" concept of beauty and truth you discussed in your last letter. Although you are quite Platonic, I find it possible to deal with this metaphysics in a metaphorical way. In all modesty, it has to be stated that, although we may speak of *metapsychology*, it does not befit us to speak of metaphysics. The latter we may well leave to those who are so well informed about the conditions in the beyond because they are on such excellent terms with it. I believe, then, that we can speak of the "metapsychological" as the hypostasis of what we infer from so-called unconscious factors in our consciousness. Seen in this light it may appear to us as if the extravert's striving is guided by a Platonic idea of "true beauty," and that of the introvert by "beautiful truth." Even in this Platonic image, however, the shadows are as missing as they are above. It will become completely human only if you assign a second "metaphysical" leading idea, that of "*ugly untruth*" to the extravert, and that of "*untrue ugliness*" to the introvert. Let us not forget the truly mythological community between Silenus-like Socrates and Plato, who was fraternally united with the beautiful Dionysus.[127] In addition, one could tell a long story about the fates of extraverts and introverts. World history is full of it. Truth and beauty do not coincide when viewed in and by themselves, but only insofar as their value for life is concerned, for the god put a knife between the two halves of the perfectly equipped and spherical primordial being.

With best regards,
your Jung

[127] In Greek mythology, Silenus, a somewhat satyr-like old man, was the teacher and companion of the god Dionysus; although ugly and mostly drunk, he was said to have had great wisdom and prophetic gifts. Plato, unlike Socrates, was regarded as good-looking by many (cf. Smith, 2003).

6 S

29. VIII. 15

Dear Friend,

Your letter gives me the impression of being very helpful in clarifying the situation.

Let me begin right away by explaining my view regarding the question of the teacher in more detail. I have always agreed to call her an ideally oriented extravert insofar as she only follows her ideal type, that is, the feeling type, or, to revert to my previous image, she is ideally oriented because she only sails. But in my view she uses a still archaic sailing boat, with which she can sail only with favorable and strong wind, and when there is no such wind, she blames the wind for not being able to get ahead. In my opinion someone is an archaic, ideally oriented extravert, then, who believes it depends on the wind, on the object, whether he is a good or poor sailor, someone who holds the object responsible and thus violates it. The ideally oriented extravert does not typically have the unpleasant quality of expecting the object to make the wind for him to sail with. This attitude is nearly always present, however, in hysterical, pathological cases, and also in coarse, uncultivated extraverts. A rather sensitive and aesthetic extravert can very well be ideally oriented, but he knows that, if he cannot go on sailing, it is not the fault of the object but of his own inability to make use of every wind current. The greater his values, the better will he be able to develop his sailing skills, and he will finally learn the art, unknown in antiquity, of "sailing against the wind." An extravert of any aesthetic sensitivity does not take possession *of the object* itself, as you write, but, just as the introvert takes possession of the *idea* of the object, the extravert takes possession of the *feeling* for the object.[128] Only

[128]This differentiation depends on the assumption that the ideal introvert has already been orienting himself to the object via the thinking function in

toward coarse or pathological extraverts is it necessary to defend the object against too much experimenting. When I state that the object is necessary for purifying the feeling, this does not mean that I advocate "predominantly experiencing the object and doing something with it."[129]

It seems to me that you feel this use of the object in a too concretistic way, and that you are not consciously aware—at least, in your feeling—of what you yourself write in your second letter: namely, that the only reason why the introvert perceives the hypothetical feeling of the extravert as a loveless experiment is that for the most part he himself can only feel concretistically. Your letter gave me the impression that your view of the extravert's "abstract" feeling differs from mine. I began using the concept of "abstract feeling" as a parallel to the introvert's "abstract thinking," in order to have a counterpart to the concrete feeling, which is more easily understood by the introvert. I am more and more under the impression that it is extraordinarily difficult for the introvert to imagine what abstract feeling is, apparently because it is not in his nature. In any case the view of the abstract feeling of the extravert expressed in your letter does not do justice to my conception of it, but rather applies to what I call concrete feeling. In my opinion, one major difference between abstract and concrete feeling is precisely that concrete feeling still "desires" the object, which abstract feeling does not, that someone who feels concretistically still thinks the wind is to blame when he

---

an introverted way, and that the ideal extravert has already been orienting himself to it using the feeling function in an extraverted way. While it is not hard to see taking possession of the idea that one has of the object as also introverted, taking possession of an originally extraverted feeling for the object does not sound like a continuation of the extraverted attachment of libido to the object but more like an introverted move. Schmid attempts to solve this confusion by reintroducing the notion of "abstract" feeling, which, from Jung's point of view, only gets him into further trouble, because abstraction is also a typically introverted move. See Jung's margin note below for what he thinks an extravert does with his feeling for the object, which does not permit abstraction from it.

[129] Jung noted in the margin: not how the extravert feels it; the other person is also to be considered.

cannot go on sailing, whereas someone who feels in an abstract way also seeks the fault in his poor sailing skills. The latter still needs the wind, however, to perfect these skills, and the object is still essential for him to purify his feelings.

I get the feeling that your image of the extraverted sailor is too archaic, and that you do not believe, for example, that he can also sail against the wind. You say, however, that the love type of the extravert is active, and that of the introvert reactive. Concrete feeling is still reactive, abstract feeling is always active. When I read your comparison of love with the feeling of hunger, I even thought you might project your more reactive type of love onto the extravert. Any extravert of some aesthetic sensitivity will agree with me that only the archaic, undeveloped loving yearning of the extravert can be compared with the desire to satisfy one's hunger. The love type of the extravert who has developed his ideal attitude to any degree at all is no longer of a reactive nature, no longer physiological; the active love type of the extravert is not, to use an expression from your book on the libido, "a longing for immediate gratification."[130] An extravert who takes any trouble at all to purify his feelings will soon realize that the concrete object will never really satisfy his yearning for love. A longing that is insatiable in the first place cannot be compared to a satiable hunger, however.[131]

Thus I must also disagree when you call the love of the extravert a striving to "achieve the fulfillment of his wish." Nor can he be satisfied by the wish fulfillment you suppose, and thus he never believes "that his object is naturally delighted by getting his love." On the contrary, extraverts with a modicum of sensitivity are afraid, so long as they have not realized their unconscious tendency toward violation, that their love might crush the object and therefore do not dare to let it become manifest. But once the extravert has realized this unconscious tendency, he sees his love not as something that

[130]This probably refers to Jung, 1911/12, § 431, where Jung writes about Cassius that he partly "reacts as a child towards his parents, always demanding love and immediate emotional rewards."

[131]The following whole paragraph is added on a separate sheet of paper.

makes the object happy but as an active force that is weakened when he wants to make someone happy with it.

I do not think that I am proceeding from a level not corresponding to reality with these views, or that I am talking of how the extravert *ought* to be, for example, while your view would correspond to who the extravert *really* is. Nor have I in mind only analyzed extraverts, for my views apply also to extraverts whose outlined attitude, and purification of their feelings, was brought about by life itself.

There is another question where our views perhaps diverge even more, namely, in what way the extravert achieves "real love," as you call it, achieves abstract feeling, and the perfection of his sailing skills. Let us once again take the example of the teacher: The way you suggest is that she would have to work her way up from the archaic attitude to real love through self-knowledge and self-reflection. I can agree with this, but in this case my view of self-knowledge is different from yours, as expressed in your letter. Self-knowledge, as you understand it, is the view on the subjective plane, the realization that the students are *also* a symbol of her power, the acknowledgement of which she tries to get from them. Achieving this self-knowledge is a purely intellectual process. In analysis you show the teacher that when she does not make any progress, it is not the wind's fault but her own; it is not because she has an archaic sailing boat but because she did not put a motor in it and cannot think; and you will be doing her a great service with your analysis in getting her to install one. So I see the usefulness of this way perfectly well—particularly for the object, the students—and I am also convinced that the teacher will benefit from it to a certain extent, at least for the moment, but I do not know if the artistically gifted teacher would choose this way. The relation between teacher and pupil is one-sided, like that of mother and daughter.

In my analyses of extraverts, particularly in cases of relations that were not one-sided (friendships, marriages, etc.), I was forced to take another way. If I show the way you suggest to a lover who is unconsciously violating his beloved, and if he follows it, his beloved will soon complain that he no longer values her, is no longer responsive to her, or only when absolutely necessary, and that his former tendency to violate, however hard to bear, at least had the advantage of liveliness. I have already experienced something of this sort, although I admit that the man in question had exaggerated the interpretation on the subjective plane. How can we explain the reaction of the beloved? In my opinion, self-knowledge, which you find necessary for the attainment of real love, never lets us find real love, but only an attitude well adapted to outer reality. For when the extravert comes to realize that when he loves somebody, he *also* loves a symbolic value of his own, an imago, a tendency in himself in the other, his feelings for the loved object will diminish considerably. He will then also want to understand his reactions toward the loved object intellectually and thus will deprive them of all spontaneity and liveliness. The wind has dropped nearly completely, and he is forced to install a motor in his boat. In this way, he has indeed adapted perfectly to external reality, but his own personality, his greatest value, his love, will become shallower, instead of deeper, by this self-knowledge.

I would probably show the teacher, and certainly an extraverted woman in love, who "breaks down in desperation over the black ingratitude" of her lover, that she still loves quite archaically, that the fault is not with the loved object (the wind), but with the fact that she has not yet sufficiently developed her ability to feel herself into the object (to sail), and that her love is purely reactive, concrete, and egocentric. Instead of getting her to install a motor in her sailing boat, I would try to further develop her natural gift for sailing. You probably remember one of our last discussions, in which I emphasized as one danger in analysis an increasing shallowness of the personality, which may be brought about by teaching the extravert to think and the introvert to feel. This [way] results in adaptation to external reality; it is of the greatest importance for our poorly adapted patients, and it is shorter than the one I proposed for the extravert, but it involves the danger of an increasing shallowness of the greatest values of the personality.

As you know, I have been occupied for months with the question of how the extravert can deepen his own personality. Here I would like to mention just a few things to you. It is also a kind of introversion, but an introversion that is completely different from that of the introvert, for it is not an act of thinking, not an intellectual process, but exclusively a matter of feeling,[132] and therefore an object is absolutely necessary for it.[133] When I say "absolutely necessary," however, I would like to emphasize once again that this should not be taken too concretistically. The object is necessary only inasmuch as feelings that are not directed toward an object are altogether unthinkable. But the object itself will not feel violated by someone who feels in an abstract way, since the latter will not demand certain feelings from the object but merely has to realize his own feelings as deeply as possible. I even know cases in which this process went ahead pretty far without the object in question noticing anything about it.

It is true that the necessary role that the object plays seems to rule out the term introversion. In your second letter you identified as the leitmotif in all misunderstandings between the two types that it is inconceivable to the extravert that the introvert can adapt to the object via abstraction. The parallel leitmotif for the introvert is that it is probably just as inconceivable to the introvert that the extravert can find his own inner reality via feeling himself into the object. And yet, in my experience, this ever-deepening realization of feelings for the object[134] is the only way for the extravert to achieve the deepening of his personality, to sail as perfectly as possible. Although it is typical for this introversion, as for any other introversion, that it leads away from outer reality (Tristan and Isolde, Romeo and Juliet, Hero and Leander, etc.), it does not

[132] Schmid describes a process that Jung would later call "introverted feeling," although Jung still downplayed the role of the object in it: introverted feeling "strives after inner intensity, for which the objects serve at most as a stimulus" (1921, § 638).

[133] The following passage, from here to the end of the paragraph, was added on a separate sheet of paper.

[134] Corrected from: this ever-deeper feeling into the object.

lead away from the loved object but, on the contrary, to an ever-deeper realization of the feelings,[135] to an ever-better utilization of the wind. So, first of all, in this process object and outer reality must not be assumed as being identical for the extravert—which is perhaps one of the points that is most difficult to grasp intellectually. In my opinion this way is a further development of the subjective change of attitude, which is the goal of Freudian analysis, as you write. Like Freudian analysis, however, the way I propose is also not that of interpreting dreams and fantasies on the subjective plane; it continues along the objective plane. To the introvert, it may make no sense that this introversion can be reached only through an analysis on the objective plane, but the object and all reactions to it are accepted as such and must not be interpreted as being also reactions to a symbol. My experience has confirmed that this is the way by which the extravert is able to work himself out of the archaic, reactive type of love, which has only concrete feelings, to an active type of love with abstract feelings.[136]

I can imagine that these remarks will make a hysterical impression on you. I also know that the way I indicated is parallel to the one our hysterical patients take in their neurosis. But this way, pathological as it may seem to the introvert, is just as imperative for the extravert for the deepening of his personality as the way that leads to his inner reality is for the introvert, which in turn seems to be schizophrenic to the extravert.[137] Perhaps many psychic illnesses could also be understood as more or less failed attempts of nature to deepen the personality. This may also be the reason why neurotics love their neu-

[135] Corrected from: to an ever-stronger feeling into the object. Lacking the conception of introverted feeling, Schmid concludes that all feelings for the object are finally extraverted, but the process he describes is one that Jungians today would call an introverted one. On Schmid on Tristan, see also 7 J and note 162.

[136] The following two paragraphs were added on a separate sheet of paper.

[137] This harks back to Jung's 1913 paper, in which he had illustrated the centrifugal and centripetal movement of the libido in extraversion and introversion by contrasting the hysteric's and schizophrenic's attitude to the external world (1913a, §§ 858–60).

rotic attitude as if it were a value that cannot be cherished highly enough.

In my last letter I called, *from my point of view*, the tendency to deepen one's own personality irrational, although I knew very well that this tendency is the rational one for the introvert. This letter should prove to you, however, that I do not want to exclude what for me is an irrational striving in favor of the rational one, and that I insist as much as you do that both the rational and the irrational be accepted.

You believe the only way the extravert can be brought to insight and self-reflection is that the object "reacts energetically," "puts up a desperate resistance," and "puts up with tastelessness and brutality, and would rather kill the other than let himself be killed." I don't believe this. The more I get to know the extravert, the more I see that one does not get anywhere with tastelessness and brutality toward him. Such an attitude on the part of the object as described by you forces the extravert, on the contrary, to summon his tendency to violation and to more and more accentuate it,[138] and finally to also give up his feelings and replace them by thinking. Certainly, as you suppose, he will thus be prepared for the struggle for adaptation and be capable of adapting better and faster also to brutal outer reality. He will not achieve a deepening of his real personality, however, through an object that reacts strongly in the way you describe. Let me add a few more remarks about this: I do not find it inconceivable that the interaction between the two different types aims at adaptation to outer reality but that, for the realization of inner reality, it is more helpful to associate with individuals of the same type.[139]

That my analyses of extraverts who are facing the problem of deepening their personalities are now, thanks to these insights, different from what I learned from you, will probably

[138] Jung noted in the margin: Thereby he realizes it.

[139] Crossed out: Although Goethe is certainly not the absolute authority for me, I cannot agree with what you write about him. What Goethe writes about the ineffectiveness of self-knowledge does perhaps not conform to your experience, but it absolutely conforms to the experience I had with myself and my extraverted friends.

not surprise you. I am thinking in particular of the problem of transference, toward which I had to adopt a new attitude in such cases. To put it briefly and schematically: Toward *extraverts* who are facing the problem of adaptation to *outer reality*, I adopt an *introverted* attitude; toward extraverts who have to *deepen their personality*, I act as an *extravert*. Toward *introverts* who have to realize their *inner reality*, I am *introverted*; toward introverts whose task is adaptation to outer reality, I am *extraverted*. Or, to carry the schematization even further: I interpret on the *objective plane* dreams and fantasies of *extraverts* that are about a *deepening of the personality*, and on the *subjective plane* dreams of extraverts that attempt an adaptation to *outer reality*. Vice versa I find that the correct interpretation for dreams of *introverts* that lead to a realization of *inner reality* is on the *subjective plane*, while I interpret dreams of introverts that suggest adaptation to *outer reality* on the *objective plane*.

I'd like to emphasize that these statements are too schematic and thus violate nature. In reality, the two opposite truths are so much intertwined that a schematic separation is always somewhat artificial. At first, I grasped these differences only intuitively in my analyses but then arrived at the abovementioned schema by keeping a check on when I intuitively preferred an interpretation on the subjective and when on the objective plane. Moreover, every dream allows for an interpretation on both the objective and the subjective plane and can thus be used for the solution of both problems, even if most dreams permit a truly meaningful interpretation only in one way.

Although Goethe is certainly not the absolute authority for me, I cannot agree with what you write about him. A man who wrote the Witch's Kitchen, the Walpurgis Night,[140] the second part of *Faust*, and the *West-Eastern Divan*[141] is in my opinion not "just as small and impotent as any other insignificant person." A genius like Goethe has a weapon in his art

[140] Two scenes in Goethe's *Faust*.
[141] A collection of poems (1819).

to look into "the ploy of secretly allied priests." The following passage in "Shakespeare and no end" shows, by the way, that he did not mistrust every kind of self-knowledge: "The highest a man can attain is becoming conscious of his own sentiments and thoughts, *knowledge of himself*,[142] which opens the way to intimate acquaintance with temperaments that are different from his own."[143] The words I quoted in my last letter refer in my view only to a certain kind of self-knowledge. Perhaps they do not correspond to *your* experience, but it is my impression that they are directed against the very thing that experience of myself and of my extraverted friends and patients has led me to mistrust, namely, a self-knowledge that is based only on intellectual self-reflection, as it springs from viewing things on the subjective plane. I therefore believe that Goethe's problem is not *only* his own personal problem but may *also* be regarded as a typical problem of the extravert.

Goethe's mistrust against self-knowledge is directed primarily against the kind of self-knowledge that believes that it no longer needs to adhere to the world in order to be attained, and that it is in possession of means that compensate for experience. Analysis, the weapon that allows us to recognize and to make proper use of the "ensnaring powers of the unconscious," acts to a certain extent as a substitute for life. But even without analysis, a healthy person is driven by his experience to unite with his unconscious, just as it happens in analysis. The great advantage of analysis, however, is that it enables us to get to know our wrong tendencies and the ensnaring powers not only through bad and painful, and very often even fatal, experiences of the object, but through a subjective experience with the help of dreams. Herein lies the greatest value of analysis, in my opinion: allowing, first, to educate sick persons to become useful individuals, persons whose experience would have never made them unite with their unconscious because of their pathological sensitivity, but

[142] Emphasis added by Schmid.
[143] Goethe, "Shakespeare and no end!" (1815).

who would have been crushed by experience. And, second, analysis allows healthy persons to realize conflicts, which otherwise would mostly have been realized only after years of experience, much more quickly and yet just as deeply, and hence to reach a much deeper union with the unconscious, effected by the experience running parallel to the analysis.

But the greatest value always harbors the greatest danger, and so here too. In my opinion the danger is that by and by an analyst might easily come to believe he could replace experience via the object by analysis—the weapon that enables him to withstand the ensnaring powers of the unconscious—or, at the most, that he will accept experience only as a "necessary evil." One might easily get to that point if one took your phrase, "life flows from ourselves, and not from the objects," too literally. I also find this too one-sided, because life also flows from the experience with the help of the object, and from the object itself. Who knows whether, for someone who acknowledges no other source of life than the source in himself, this source will not dry up sooner or later (depending on the source's strength). The object not only has effects that have a corrective influence and thus further our development but also has a fertilizing effect. I think one of the dangers for someone who is advanced in his analysis is his belief that he could replace not only the corrective influence of the object, which is so unbearably painful to him, but also its fertilizing effect by the knowledge of his unconscious, thus removing himself further and further from life.

The extravert must learn, however, that there is life also in himself, and not only in the object, and that the latter can *only* fertilize him, but will not bear children in his stead. The introvert must learn for his part that there is life not only in himself but also in the object, and that he cannot bear children without being fertilized by the object. If he cannot do this, he may well be able to lay eggs but will try in vain to hatch a living being from them. The extravert, to stay with this image, can be compared to the hen that wants to be perpetually fertilized and may well sit on the nest to hatch an egg but forgets that it has not laid one yet.

In my opinion, the way suggested by you, namely, to bring the extravert to real love, will actually lead to an activation of his shadow (his thinking), and the result could easily be that twilight will spread everywhere in his soul. I regret that in my previous letter, after having assembled an airplane out of the sailing and the motor boat, I did not mention one idea because it seemed self-evident to me. This idea is that nobody can fly in the air for long; just like *Antaeus,* he will always have to come back to Mother Earth to renew his strength.[144] Flying, or turning one's shadow into light, to use your words, is an ideal state. It remains a wishful delirium that Hephaestus will weld the two halves of the primordial being together again, as Plato describes it.[145] In my view, however, twilight will spread everywhere only when a motor is built into the sailing boat, and a sail added to the motorboat, without perfecting the sails into wings, and the propelling screw into a propeller—in other words, when one imagines to have attained the ideal. I think that, except perhaps for a few moments, we cannot reach the ideal state in life at all. We can purify our thinking and our feeling only alternately, one after the other, by directing our energy to the one or to the other. But this will enable us, after all, to rise above the water in those rare moments. Perhaps never completely, and perhaps it is just as well, because from the moment we have attained an ideal it ceases to be one. And from the moment we no longer have an ideal,

[144] In Greek mythology Antaeus, son of Poseidon and Gaia, was a giant who was strong as long as he remained in contact with the earth (i.e., his mother Gaia) but became weak once he was lifted into the air.

[145] Hephaestus was the Greek god of technology, blacksmiths, craftsmen, artisans, sculptors, metals, metallurgy, fire, and volcanoes; he was seen as the blacksmith of the gods. "Now, supposing Hephaestus were to come and stand over them with his tool bag as they lay there side by side, and suppose he were to ask, 'Tell me, my dear creatures, what do you really want with one another?' And suppose they didn't know what to say, and he went on, 'How would you like to be rolled into one, so that you could always be together, day and night, and never be parted again? Because if that's what you want, I can easily weld you together, and then you can live your two lives in one' " (*Symposium*, in Plato, 1961, p. 545). See also note 123.

all growth, all striving, all development, and all life are gone, and with them the possibility of salvation, for:

> He who keeps forever striving,
> Him can we redeem.[146]

So it is a good thing that "the god put a knife between the two halves of the perfectly equipped and spherical primordial being."

I feel sorry for the man, however, who loses his faith in the ideal because the intellect or experience has shown him that knife. The torments of Tantalus await him.[147]

With best regards,
your Hans Schmid

I would be grateful to you for a typed copy of this letter, and if possible also of my last one.

[146] Goethe, *Faust*, part 2, act 5.

[147] According to Greek mythology, Tantalus was welcomed to Zeus's table, but stole ambrosia and nectar, revealed the secrets of the gods, committed perjury, and killed his son and served him as a meal to the gods. His punishment—now a proverbial term for temptation without satisfaction (cf. "to tantalize")—was to stand in the river Eridanos beneath fruit trees with low branches. Whenever he reached for the fruit, the branches raised it from his grasp, and whenever he bent down to get a drink, the water receded before he could get any.

7 J

4 Sept. 1915

Dear Friend,

When two opposed types discuss the type problem, the greatest part of the discussion is taken up by talking and understanding at cross-purposes. Language here reveals its incredible incapacity of reflecting the finer nuances that are indispensable for understanding. Thus, when it comes to matters of psychology, every linguistic sign can mean both one thing and its opposite. When you speak of the extravert and the feeling of an "identité mystique,"[148] then naturally many things I said about the extravert do not apply. What I was actually talking about was the "ideally oriented" extravert, and by "ideal" I do not mean "ideal" in the sense it is used in expressions such as "ideal aspirations" and "ideal convictions," but "ideal" in the sense of "corresponding to one's principle." Here the term "ideal" also implies that the ideal type is an *imaginary* or *abstracted* type that does not exist in reality, because a real person naturally also has the other mechanism within himself, with the help of which he can take the edge off what is all-too sharp in the "ideal." The more "ideal" a case is the more pathological it is. You are perfectly right, therefore, in assuming that I am speaking mainly of "coarse" or "pathological" persons, among whom the "ideally oriented" can be found. The term "ideal" lays an unintentional mantrap. In contrast to these cases, you are speaking of the *compensated* ones, where the situation is of course different. But then again you are mainly speaking of how a case "should be," and not how it "is," whereas I proceeded from the assumption that we were talking about the "types" themselves, and not about "compensated"

[148] Mystical identity, a term coined by Lévy-Bruehl; cf. "participation mystique."

cases, in which the type problem is actually harder to identify in my opinion than in pure cases. But anyway, since you have shifted this to a discussion of the compensated case, I will go along with this different program.

On this basis, my judgement about experiencing via the object is of course no longer valid, because with the help of compensation the extravert can very easily "realize" his feeling via the object without violating it in the least. This "realization" is a process taking place within the subject, and so much inwardly that the object, as you rightly say, often does not notice it at all. Now this is precisely what I call the "view on the subjective plane." This realization proceeds from compensation, but not according to the *principle* of this type, for extraversion goes outward to the object, and not inward into the subject, which is introversion. The realization of the feeling goes to the subject and is thus a process of introversion. At the same time it is also a thinking process, however, since realization means that I juxtapose the feeling as an object, differentiating myself from it.[149] Without this differentiation, I am not able to see what is happening, for then, being indistinguishable from it, I will be the process itself. "Realization," as the term already implies, is an "*objectivation*" of the process, without which apperception is not possible at all. This apperception of the process is the attainment of *self-knowledge* or, in other words, the *view on the subjective plane*.

Abstract feeling, being of a hypothetical nature like all abstraction, is not a violent action in itself. Taken as a feeling in itself, abstract feeling is a virtue and supreme refinement, just like the abstract thinking of the introvert. Its violent character is revealed only in its influence on the object. That is why we must let the object have the last word in this matter. When I violate the extravert with my abstract thinking, this is a fact, and this fact cannot be dismissed even if I insist that the other is merely thinking concretistically. In this case he has the last

[149] Jung, unlike Schmid in the previous letter, does not yet conceive of an introverted feeling process.

word, and I will have to realize that I have to be careful with my virtue so as to avoid harm. Abstract thinking and feeling are not violent in themselves, nor do we experience them as such, because civilized man has long unlearned to attribute his various complaints to the pressure of domestication. On closer consideration, however, abstraction in itself is also an act of violence against the disparate phenomenon. For in order to achieve abstraction, we pour what is separate and manifold into a flask, heat it up, and melt it, and thus force the volatility of the matter into the template. In that way we create a *spiritus*, which is an abstraction.[150] The elements in the flask complain about violent treatment, because for them distillation runs counter to their nature. We often forget how we achieved our virtues and take our achievements for granted, thinking they would be a blessing for others, too. (Cf. the Negroes and the blessings of civilization. Good examples of this are the Negro republics, and the exemplary social dignity of the Negro in the United States: "for colored people only"[151]—naturally.) Of course, it is the horse's fault if it cannot pull a railway train; why is it so weak! Someone could point out, however, that a man who harnesses a horse to a railway train is committing an act of violence and is an idiot to boot. What I want to say is that the explanation for the question of violence cannot be found only in what is pitiably concretistic.

You have complicated the matter considerably by basing the discussion on the compensated type. But since I am letting myself be "stimulated by the object," I will try to do justice also to the complicated situation.

We surely agree in assuming that the "coarse," "pathological," or "ideally oriented" extravert violates the object by his direct and exclusive relation to it. This crude form of violence naturally disappears to the extent the extravert abstracts his feeling, by which the latter becomes spiritualized, which is a

[150]This is one of Jung's earliest uses of an alchemical "operation" as an analogy for a psychical process. The operation he describes here is known to alchemical practice as *sublimatio* (cf. Jung, 1935/36[1943], e.g., § 511). Cf. Edinger, 1985, pp. 116–45.

[151]This expression in English in the original.

true sublimation process ("from one bride-bed to another harried").[152]

There are things to which we cannot do justice completely with abstract thinking, and which we even violate if we subject them to abstract thinking. Equally there are things that must not be subjected to abstract feeling. Someone like the pure type, who has advanced from the crude to the *secondary* state, that is, to the abstraction of his adaptive organ, is nevertheless still capable of violence, but in a more refined and all the more cruel way, in that the introvert forces everything to fit into his intellectual pattern, and the extravert into the emotional one, since both of them are rationalists in their whole structure, even though they affect the contrary. When the two meet they are a perfect match so long as they do not try to understand each other psychologically. Everything will be fine, for instance, when the hardships of life make such heavy demands on them that they have to direct most of their concentration to the struggle for existence, and therefore cannot make any efforts to assert themselves as individual beings. When there is no longer such immediate necessity, however, so that they turn to look at one another, they are convinced that they have never understood each other. The intellect of the one comes up against the other's concretistic "representation," which he finds utterly disagreeable, and the feeling of the latter comes up against the other's concretistic "sensation," which he finds equally disagreeable. Then, at best, there follows savior-like suffering, an educating, coercing, correcting, "fathering," and "mothering" of the other, heroic feats of love of nearly inestimable proportions. And then comes the well-known story of the Jew without a train ticket, whom the conductor wanted to throw out at every stop. When a passenger

[152] A quote from *Faust* on the alchemical process: "*Das Widrige zusammengoß. / Da ward ein roter Leu, ein kühner Freier, / Im lauen Bad der Lilie vermählt, / Und beide dann mit offnem Flammenfeuer / Aus einem Brautgemach ins andere gequält*" (He sought the opposing powers to blend. / Thus, a red lion, a bold suitor, married / The silver lily, in the lukewarm bath, / And, from one bride-bed to another harried, / The two were seen to fly before the flaming wrath). Goethe, 1832, part 1, lines 1042–45.

finally asked him: "Where are you actually going to?" the poor man replied: "To Karlsbad—if my constitution can stand it."[153]

The mistake that is being made is quite obvious: *each wants to better the other*. This is the objective plane of viewing things. This missionary attitude is all very Christian but is extremely annoying to the introvert. He will kick the missionary out. The extravert's reaction is very clearly demonstrated in your letter: in your opinion, it would be a mistake if we wanted to teach the extravert to think, and the introvert to feel. You maintain the opposite standpoint, namely, to let things be and, at most, further one's innermost tendency—thinking in the introvert, and feeling in the extravert. As you so accurately describe it for the case of the extravert, this leads to "realization," which is nothing else but *thinking* about feeling. This is how he learns thinking. You have witnessed a famous case of this kind, in which a distinguished extravert was put, by an introvert *de pur sang*,[154] into the saddle that is so characteristic of the extravert, on which he then galloped off to those adventures in which he learned to "realize."[155] This was not taught to him. He learned it by himself, because he had no other choice. This is precisely—and pray forgive me—viewing things on the subjective plane. As you told me,[156] however, a certain other extravert tried to directly impose thinking on the former, which he took very much amiss, as we know, just as an introvert worth his salt will resist with might and main all attempts from the outside to impose and force feeling on him. The dignity of man—an essential notion still to be learned by all missionaries!

It is a remarkable fact that the more you develop the extravert's feeling, believing to thus enhance your feeling into the

[153]This was also a favorite joke of Freud's, quoted, for example, in his *Interpretation of Dreams* (1900a, p. 195). Jung's version misses one point, namely, that each time tickets were inspected the man was taken out of the train and treated more and more severely. Karlsbad was a famous spa, of course.

[154]French for "pure-blooded."

[155]Jung is obviously referring to Schmid and himself, probably to an interaction in Schmid's analysis (see the introduction).

[156]"As you told me" inserted later.

object, the less the object is actually comprehended, for the object requires not only to be felt into but also sensation and thinking. The latter two cannot, as we know, on any account be replaced by feeling-into. That is why raising the level of feeling leads, as you correctly say, to a feeling-into the subject, as the necessary exaggeration of the feeling makes the subject's lack of activity in thinking and sensation felt. Gently but persistently, this vacuum sucks the libido back from feeling-into and thereby enforces "realization," which, as I have already emphasized, is precisely viewing things on the subjective plane.

I completely agree with your supposition that the missionary activity the two types exercise on one another leads not to a deepening of the personality at all but *only* to a good adaptation to reality. I have always defended this principle, namely, that one should not proselytize the other but should give him the opportunity to grow from what is his very own. In my humble opinion, the famous case of a certain extravert quoted above[157] is a good example of this; at the same time this case is probably evidence of the fact that there is no essential[158] difference between your method and mine on this point.

When you say that the act of "deepening of the personality" has merely to do with feeling, you obviously see only the dynamic side of the process, that is, the progress in the development of love. But you are forgetting that it is precisely "realization" through which a deepening of the personality is achieved. "Realizing" is an introverting process, an objectification; it is gaining insight, making something conscious, understanding, hence an *intellectual* process. Someone who, without "realizing," always continued to fly on the wings of his feeling, would be, and remain to be, an incurably extraverted "dud." It is just as typical of the extravert to underestimate and fail to notice his own introversion process, as it is of the introvert to underestimate and fail to notice his extraversion process.

[157] "of a certain extravert quoted above" inserted later.

[158] Corrected from: real.

So long as the extravert only feels but does not realize,[159] he will naturally have a very inadequate relation to the object, and that is why his "object" will not correspond to reality at all, but will be a subjective fantasy. Someone who just feels does not think, but fantasizes. Through feeling-into, the fantasy is *transferred* or projected into the "object," but the actual object is thus distorted. If the object is endowed with reason, it will clearly see that it represents merely a fantasy to the other. When the other finally understands the real nature of the object, he cools off considerably. This naturally offends the object, particularly if it was hoping to get something from the extravert's feeling, and it will feel disappointed and deceived. It is exactly as if a very scientifically oriented doctor treated a patient, who expects to be cured, in a theoretically absolutely correct manner, and then, when the cure finally fails, explained to the patient that "in theory" he would actually have to be cured by now. I can understand the patient when he assumes that he has simply served as a guinea pig for a theory, that is, for a scientific fantasy. The progress of scientific theory is certainly a great and noble thing, but there seem to be good reasons why experiments are conducted with guinea pigs rather than with humans.[160]

In a refined person, the violent act has only become more refined, which just makes it that bit more devilish. Therefore, you are quite correct in saying that the way indicated by you runs parallel to that of a neurosis, that is, to the way of the "coarse" and "pathological" extravert.

It nearly seems to me as if you were still of the opinion that, for example, I would analyze dreams on the subjective plane only. Since I cannot provide you with evidence from my ongoing analyses, as you know nothing about them, I must revert to that famous case mentioned above, in which you have witnessed my method—which you suggest in your letter—put into practice. The relation to the object that resulted from that

[159] Struck out: whereby he comes to thinking and sensing.

[160] The following paragraph was added in the margin.

analysis[161] seems to have had a not inconsiderable influence on the further course the development of this extravert took. He has often been heard talking of Tristan and Iseult,[162] of Faust and Helen, etc.

It is a well-known fact that man is also capable of accepting something as true without having seen it with his eyes and touched it with his hands. It is this truly human capacity that spares him a number of highly unpleasant experiences. The average person seems to be satisfied, for example, by the theoretical reasoning that it is dangerous to stick his head out of an elevator on its way up. He does not need to get his head torn off for the sake of experience. It would also be a rather daring undertaking for someone to actually try out and see if it were really morally impossible for him to commit a murder. There are a great many things that cannot, or need not, be experienced via the object.[163] For all these things we need the symbolic view on the subjective plane—if, that is, these tendencies are not to succumb irretrievably to repression again. But when an actual experience via the object is possible, or even indicated, only a completely fatuous person would want to enforce a symbolic and subjective interpretation. I guess you do not count me among such pigheaded solipsists; it would also run counter to what you have experienced.

As far as the behavior of the object toward the violence of the extravert is concerned, to which you object, you are[164] thinking completely extravertedly about it, and are suppress-

[161] Here Jung speaks directly of an "analysis" as the situation in which Schmid witnessed his method.

[162] See 6 S. On 6 May and 29 May 1916, Schmid presented a paper on Tristan at the Society for Analytical Psychology (*Protokolle* etc.). In the discussion, Jung and Schmid again took up their discussion on types, also with regard to the role of an interpretation on the subjective or objective plane for thinking or feeling processes. Cf. also Maria Moltzer's comment that the paper's "essential feature lies in the conflict between the individuation and the collective principles and its possible solution through the Transcendental Function" (in Shamdasani, 1998a, p. 102).

[163] Struck out: in order to protect oneself.

[164] Struck out: naturally.

ing the object anew. You really cannot dictate to the object how it ought to react, and which reaction would be the right one. Such good intentions may be appropriate among extraverts but not in the relation between the types. *I must emphasize that an introvert reacts in just the way I said.* This is what happens and what is. The introvert couldn't care less if this has any effect at all on the extravert, because he is no extravert who worries about such effects.[165] I am talking about what is, and not about what would be desirable. When the introvert reacts accordingly to how he is blindly attacked and abused as a fantasy by the other, he forces him, as you rightly say, to consciously bring out his tendency toward violation, which makes the extravert finally realize that he has such a tendency. He forces him to give up his feelings—yes, he does—and then the extravert is forced to start thinking. In that way he achieves, and here you are right again, adaptation to reality, which cannot be accomplished without thinking and sensation. Once he has achieved adaptation, he at last has his hands free for his own use. He can then try out his violence and his feeling-into on himself for a change in order to deepen his personality. His former extraversion to the object was so exaggerated because his adaptation to it was so highly inadequate. The deficit forced him to make ever-greater expenditures. Once adaptation is achieved, his libido can turn inward. Of course, the introvert never fancies that by his self-defense he is deepening the other's personality, nor does he defend himself for this reason; he really does it only not to be destroyed himself. It is only the extravert who can see this in a different light, as he is convinced from the outset that he has the other's best interest in mind, and that everything he does is beneficial for the other's well-being. This role of the savior is infantile humbug and has to be nailed down as such.

In my opinion, you have touched upon something very important with your idea that an association of like types is more conducive to a deepening of one's own personality than an association of different types. Just as I am absolutely con-

[165] Struck out: He does not worry about that.

vinced that it is mandatory for adaptation to reality that the two opposed types confront each other unreservedly, I also believe that a deepening of the personality, with all its irrational values, can take place only by associating with the same type. Interference of the opposite type is certainly a painful disturbance, for everything that represents the highest meaning and value for the one side is utmost nonsense and without value for the other. The directions of the irrational psychological processes are actually diametrically opposed. What the extravert calls *human* is just "all too human" for the introvert. What the introvert calls *human* is airy and gaseous for the other. This discrepancy makes it quasi impossible for the two, because of the irritating difference in tone, to go together in the irrational[166] developmental process. It is another question whether the irrational process in the opposed types does not bring to light a product that is equally valuable to each of them, although the values they find in it are opposed to one another.

This question must be left open for the time being.

I find your schema of attitudes of the analyst disagreeable, because I myself could never adopt something like this. I am as I am, and that also in analysis. I do not know whether it is necessary for the extravert to play a role, nor do I know whether I may not unconsciously play a role myself—after all, one can never know things like that. I would not be surprised to find, however, that it may be the specific task of the extravert, in his feeling attitude toward the other, to make appropriate corrections in the object in order to eliminate his typical violence. Certainly the introvert has to do something similar in the intellectual sphere. As the case may be, he must be either reserved or forthcoming with his thoughts. I would not know at all how to tune in to the individual task of the patient—for how could I be so vain as to know what his task is? I would feel sorry for a patient whose task I thought I knew a priori,

[166] Again, this word, here, does not mean what it came to mean in *Psychological Types* (cf. Jung, 1921, § 774). Cf. above, where Jung wrote of the "irrational (that is, psychological) truth."

or at least more or less in advance, because then I would be on my best way to be giving that sort of counseling that the Freudian school has always imputed to me. Nothing can be done against projections, however.

If in my last letter I talked primarily about the inferior extravert, you talk about the inferior introvert when it comes to matters of self-knowledge. Without doubt, there is a danger of cheating ourselves out of a really full life by philosophizing. I have a very tolerant attitude toward such people, however, because in my experience there are quite a number of people who are rendered relatively harmless by contenting themselves with a surrogate of life. There are also such useless and objectionable seeds in man that living a half life, which leaves these seeds undeveloped, is by far preferable to their full development. I am not inclined to believe in man as a *unum et bonum et perfectum.*[167] Hence, I'm also against proselytizing—unless it is for monism, abstinence, the Salvation Army, pacifism, or the YMCA.[168]

So whoever turns the idea of self-knowledge into a pseudo-idea, and fraudulently abuses it to escape himself, has probably good reasons to do so. An honest man, who also has a certain amount of courage, will never use self-knowledge as a surrogate for life. His nature would not permit it.

But as we all are deficient in a certain sense, namely, when measured against an ideal, self-knowledge does actually serve us not to commit a number of wrongs and stupidities, which would inevitably follow from the deficiency of our nature.

I am sorry to have attacked my beloved Goethe in my last letter with regard to his statement about self-knowledge. True, it was very disrespectful, but all the same I did have a point in taking the *verba magistri*[169] not too seriously, since Goethe himself has provided the rebuttal of his own position as shown by the beautiful quote in your last letter. It is difficult to argue with such masters, because in their honesty they always state

[167] Latin for "(someone who is) one and good and perfect."

[168] In the original: *christliche Jünglingsvereine* = Christian associations of young men.

[169] Latin for "the words of the master."

also the respective opposite somewhere else. Just think of Goethe's diametrically opposed statements on women! The words of the fathers are a fine thing—so long as we do not use them as arguments.

It follows from all this that your criticism of self-knowledge refers to a concept that is actually a caricature[170] of its real meaning. This inferior concept has nothing to do with what I called the view on the subjective plane. But I acknowledge your right to stress the existence of an inferior concept and use of self-knowledge just as emphatically[171] as I underlined and defended the existence of a concretistic perception of extraverted feeling operations. Toward the other, one tends to take a position based on our experience on a par with the average of previous incidences and is little inclined to trust him[172] a priori to really have the more perfect in mind. The experience of what goes on around us every day has made us so cold, however, that we still do not expect anything good to come out of Nazareth.[173] The less we are trusting each other, the more proofs we get that this trust is indeed unjustified.

It seems to me that we might now have reached an agreement on this point, after having exposed our mutual mistrust—based on unshakable experience—so emphatically.

So let me turn to another point in which I differ from your view, or rather from what your written words (sic!)[174] say. The difference[175] starts with your idea that "genius" would be a weapon against the unconscious. It would be easy to demonstrate that genius also offers the greatest opportunities of falling victim to the powers of the unconscious. Genius is both: the capacity to unlock the unconscious, and the capacity to

[170] Corrected from: which is an inferior caricature.

[171] Corrected from: energetically.

[172] Corrected from: to give the other the credit.

[173] "And Nathanael said unto him, Can there any good thing come out of Nazareth? Philip saith unto him, Come and see" (John 1:46; King James Version). Jung repeatedly referred to this passage in his work (1921, § 438; 1935/36[1943], § 126; 1955, CW § 344, n. 685, GW § 336, n. 699; 1957, § 567).

[174] "(sic!)" added later.

[175] Corrected from: discussion.

give its elements a visible form. In the very rare case this operation is successful without destroying the person in question (and you know how rarely this happens), we suddenly believe that genius is a superb weapon against the ensnaring powers of the unconscious. But in the more frequent case that these very capacities devour the person who has them and lead to an untimely death or lingering illness, we believe that genius is also a terrible snare. I tend to think that the number of geniuses is not all that inconsiderable, but that the number of those who are not destroyed by their genius is infinitesimal. It does not help to say that it is precisely those few who are the "true" geniuses, while the ones who were destroyed had not been true geniuses in the first place. When we know how thin the thread is, on which the sword above the head of the genius is suspended,[176] we can only say: this one has barely managed to escape by the skin of his teeth, and the other did not make it by a hair's breadth. Even the so-called true genius carries wounds close to his thread of life. Thus, genius is a terrible double-edged weapon, which always inflicts wounds on both sides, a bit more gravely here, a bit more lightly there. Neither the genius nor the average person can get through life unscathed, but only the genius is affected to a much, much higher degree.

Genius is as little a substitute for analysis as "experience." A "healthy person" is never driven by his experience "to unite with his unconscious." With this view you would deny analysis the right to exist altogether. According to your view the significance of analysis seems to be limited to a psychological technique that, for pathologically sensitive people, is a partial substitute for a life they find impossible to lead, and which offers healthy people some help in coping with their conflicts. In the former case, analysis serves as the dressing of a wound; in the latter, as a motor oil. I readily concede that even great Caesar might have found it necessary to stop up a bung hole somewhere,[177] and that the halls in the Louvre offer an excel-

[176] The reference is to the proverbial "Sword of Damocles" that hung over the head of Damocles, supported by only a hair.

[177] Struck out: and that the great pyramid is a sudorific. Cf. Hamlet, act 5, scene 1: "Why may not imagination trace the noble dust of Alexander, till he

lent opportunity for "physical exercise,"[178] but I deny that this is Caesar's or the Louvre's "greatest value." I am more than ready to acknowledge and admire all the useful things that make life possible and easier, but that the usefulness of a work of culture should be its "highest value" is completely beyond me. As I do not want to immediately sin against my above-mentioned principle of implicit trust, I assume that what you really meant was that this is precisely *not* its highest value.

If this so highly praised experience alone would suffice, what would then be the point of science and other cultural achievements, with all their intrinsic values beyond the question of usefulness?

Someone who in his experience also experiences his unconscious has by no means united with it—unless, that is, he *knows* it. The process of attaining knowledge covers many fields and is possible only with the help of those formulas that have been elaborated and handed down by the history of ideas over several millennia. This treasure trove is called science, without which knowledge is impossible. An animal lives its unconscious, and is completely united, even identical, with it. What is missing is only knowledge, seeing things from the subject's point of view. In this knowledge—that is, in what analysis is in itself, regardless of its usefulness—lies its "greatest value"; its true value is that it is a standpoint beyond experience, out of the reach of the rationalistic intentions of those who want to make it the servant of their own incompetence.

When somebody says: "Love thy neighbor as thyself,"[179] the meaning of this statement lies in the ideal of Christian love, and not in the thought that it is also of the greatest practical value to raise this Machiavellian principle of "*do ut des*"[180] to a religious ideal. Similarly, it would be a grave injustice against the spirit of the achievement that we call analysis to

find it stopping a bung-hole?" and: "Imperious Caesar, dead and turn'd to clay, might stop a hole to keep the wind away."

[178] This expression is in English in the original.

[179] Leviticus 19:18.

[180] Latin for "I give so that you give," a Roman saying and maxim.

limit its highest value to its usefulness for our lives. Seen in the light of day, it is also clear that it could not provide this practical service at all if it did not have precisely the value I emphasized. "Life is not the highest of goods,"[181] and least of all that which cures a few neurotics and shortens some conflicts for a few healthy people.

But lest you arrive at the opinion that I underestimate the practical usefulness of analysis, let me conclude by saying that I am as skeptical of knowledge without usefulness, as I am of usefulness without well-founded knowledge. Knowledge without usefulness adorns philosophical chessboards and produces fat volumes for venerable libraries. Usefulness without meaning fills pockets and the churches of Christian Science. The value of analysis, however, is not only that it is of practical use but that it is also a living knowledge in and by itself. Thinking is life just as much as doing is. Thinking is not merely a "realization" of life; life can also be a "realization" of thinking.

As to your concluding remark, I really must add for the sake of poetic justice that I did not invent that legend of the sailing-motor-airplane-monster, but that by alluding to the Platonic myth I only wanted to emphasize, ever so delicately, that this monster is hardly viable, precisely because of its ideal nature. I hardly believe that I will go to the hell that has so very amiably been intended for me, only because I find the sailing-motor-airplane-dragon an impossible ideal. Surely Sisyphus was an idealist, wasn't he?

With best regards,
your Jung

[181] "Das Leben ist der Güter Höchstes nicht, / Der Übel Größtes aber ist die Schuld" (Life is not the highest of goods, / But the greatest of evils is guilt); the final words in Friedrich Schiller's drama, *Die Braut von Messina* (*The Bride of Messina*).

28. IX. 15

Dear Friend,

It is not in the character of the extravert to be distrustful. As long as he still considers his thinking infallible, he will be distrustful toward the thoughts of the other in his thinking. But in most cases the extravert has still to learn how to be distrustful in his feelings.

You read a mistrust into my last letter that wasn't there, and you speak, therefore, of *mutual* mistrust. I did grant you the *a priori* trust you postulated in your letter, and thus my first reaction when reading it was being greatly astounded that you took a large part of my remarks personally, and adopt an attitude toward them like someone who defends himself against someone distrustful.

In the first part of my letter, in which I wrote only about the psychology of the extravert, I tried to set forth my views on the latter's problems, and to stress particularly those points in which my views do not agree with yours. I was far from wanting to lecture you, let alone to reform you. I simply felt the need to explain what I see as my truth. I admit that there were times when I believed that the introvert would have to take the same way as the extravert to realize his feelings. I have long since reached the conclusion, however, that such processes—if he has to go through them at all—are of much less importance to the introvert for the realization of his feelings, much as the classical languages are less important to a doctor than to a philologist. For the extravert these processes are indispensable for the development of his personality; for the introvert they are indispensable only insofar as he *also* wants to develop his feeling side,[182] and[183] I am far from claiming that

[182] Here again, the feeling side of the introvert is assumed by Schmid (following Jung's original equation of feeling and extraversion) to be extraverted—even if mostly undeveloped, because in the unconscious.

[183] Rest of sentence beginning with "and" inserted later.

this development will necessarily follow exactly the same course as in the extravert.

In the second part of my letter, in the discussion on self-knowledge, I tried to emphasize the dark sides of a self-knowledge that is based exclusively on intellectual knowledge, and I had inferior introverts—as you call them—in mind. I would never have believed that you felt that this concerned you. In my last sentence I expressly thought of an introverted poet whom I am treating at the moment, a true Tantalus,[184] who is still so much of an idealist that he cannot let go of his suffering, but who has lost any viable faith in his ideal in the process. Thus I was far from amiably intending that "hell" for you. For the time being, I do not want to enter into the discussion of the value of the genius; it seems to me that we, or at least I, still lack the psychological basis for discussing such an extraordinarily difficult problem. As far as I can see, I must say, however, that I am not convinced by your arguments.

I offered my schema of the analyst's attitudes only as an illustration of my views that "violates nature," and I ask you to believe me that I don't abuse it as a brute of a coachman does his horses. I, too, do not want to play a role in analysis. As I pointed out, it was by intuition, not by wanting to represent anything, that I came to make the appropriate corrections concerning my attitude, which is peculiar to my type only. I, too, do not *know* in advance the task a patient is confronted with, but I often *feel* intuitively that a dream is rather suggesting such and such a task to be solved, and—without representing anything—I adopt an attitude according to this feeling.

I am not surprised that my concept of self-knowledge seems like a caricature to you. For my feeling, though not for my thinking, your concept of self-knowledge is just as much of a caricature. In my opinion, it was against this caricature of self-knowledge, as I understand it, that the words of "father" Goethe, quoted in the last but one letter, were directed.[185] I dis-

[184] See 6 S, note 147.

[185] Cf. the discussion on Goethe's authority in 6 S and 7 J.

pute that my conception of self-knowledge is inferior, as such, as you say. I know it has to be inferior to you, just as yours is to me. I can understand, however, that for you your concept is the only correct and valuable one.

I think we have given a fine example of talking and understanding at cross-purposes in the last two letters regarding the concepts of *value* and *usefulness*. I concede that the few words with which I described the value of analysis were perhaps clumsy, and in any case did not adequately express what I wanted to say. But I am amazed that you can state,[186] just on the basis of this single sentence, that analysis is only a psychological technique to me, a dressing and a motor oil.[187] If you are able to get at least a vague idea of my life over the past years, you will have to realize that analysis had to be more to me than a technique, or even the best of psychic motor oils. As an extravert, when I speak about the value of something, I do not mean its usefulness. You yourself once put one important difference between the two types roughly as follows: for the introvert, the value of a thing lies only in its usefulness at the moment; for the extravert, the value of the thing lies in itself. You are right, therefore, in trusting me not to think that the highest value of analysis lies in its usefulness. For when I write, for instance, that analysis allows the healthy person to achieve a much deeper union with the unconscious than would be possible without it, I am having things in mind that are no longer reconcilable with the principle of utilitarianism at all, and which are quite different from what you call "some help in coping with conflicts," or even the "shortening of some conflicts." I find it "business-like"[188] and an outright devaluation to speak of the *usefulness* of, for example, religion, art, or love. I'd rather like to inquire into the *values* these three manifestations of life have for life.

When I speak of the *highest* value of analysis, I am thinking of values such as those of the Louvre, which are debased when

[186] Corrected from: can accuse me.

[187] Here one sentence is heavily struck out.

[188] This expression in English in the original—alluding to Jung's use of it in 1 J.

its halls are used only for "physical exercise."[189] For me value does not mean usefulness; utility can be measured, whereas a value can only be estimated. The highest value, therefore, is something immensurable [*sic*][190] to me. In my opinion, analysis has such an immensurable [*sic*] value. I think it is a manifestation of life, a life principle, which can perhaps be seen as a parallel to the principles mentioned above (religion, art, love), and which, like all life principles, consequently has an *immanent*,[191] and hence (because it cannot be quantitatively compared) incommensurable [*sic*], value. But in calling something a life principle, I am referring to the highest possible value I can imagine.

This brings us to a further difference in our views: while you speak of the usefulness of analysis for life, I would like to speak of its value for life. For me, life and every life principle have an immanent[192] value, beyond usefulness and knowledge, which I can only estimate with the help of my feeling, and which, as I feel it, cannot be known through any form of knowledge, be it as deep as it may, because this value is on a higher level than knowledge. I believe, by the way, that your opinion on that is not that much different, because you, too, acknowledge that there are things to which one cannot do full justice with abstract thinking (which knowledge surely is).[193] *For me*, analysis is also such a thing. The highest value of a religion, of a work of art, or of love, can never be perceived through knowledge (in general? or perhaps only through my knowledge?).[194] The experiences of all theoretical studies of art and religion, which as we know deprive these principles of all life, lead me to assume that the value of analysis can never be grasped by a science at all. I can understand very well that

[189] This expression in English in the original, again alluding to Jung (7 J).

[190] Original: *etwas immensurables*—a nonexistent word, which Jung promptly corrected to *incommensurables* ("incommensurable") in the margin.

[191] Struck out by Jung, and replaced by "transcendent" in the margin.

[192] As above.

[193] Here Jung made a big question mark in the margin.

[194] Jung highlighted the following two sentences and wrote "gnosis" in the margin.

for you the value of analysis lies in being "a living knowledge in and by itself," because for you thinking is life, as you write. For me thinking is something dead, even something deadly for life; for me feeling is life, and life can also be a realization of feeling.[195] When I do that "extra piece of work," however, as Schiller once so aptly stated in Goethe's case (letter to Goethe, 23 August 1794),[196] when I take a thinking and intellectual stance toward the world, I can very well imagine that thinking, too, can be life. I know, however, that I am not following my true nature with this attitude. For me the highest value of analysis does not lie in knowledge—in which there lies a potentially deadly danger in my opinion—but *for me* its highest value lies in the life principle contained in it, which can be measured only by way of feeling.[197] It follows that, despite your statement to the contrary, I must maintain that life can be a substitute for analysis, and this without doing "grave injustice to the spirit of analysis." On the contrary, this is the highest valuation of a work I can give.

Similarly, I must uphold another statement made in my last letter. I wrote that, although the extravert's realization of feelings is a kind of introversion, it is not an act of thinking or an intellectual process, like the introversion of the introvert, but purely a matter of feeling.[198] You counter this statement with the opposite one: "The realization of feelings is a thinking

[195] The following two sentences were added on separate sheet of paper.

[196] In context, the quote reads as follows: *Aber diese logische Richtung, welche der Geist bei der Reflexion zu nehmen genötigt ist, verträgt sich nicht wohl mit der ästhetischen.... Sie hatten also eine Arbeit mehr: denn so wie Sie von der Anschauung zur Abstraktion übergingen, so mußten Sie nun rückwärts Begriffe wieder in Intuitionen umsetzen und Gedanken in Gefühle verwandeln, weil nur durch diese das Genie hervorbringen kann.* (But this logical direction, which the intellect is forced to take in reflection, cannot easily be reconciled with the aesthetic one.... So you had to do an extra piece of work: for just as you went from perception to abstraction, you now, reversely, had to make concepts into intuitions, and change thoughts into feelings, because it is only through the latter that the genius can create.) (Schiller & Goethe, 1905).

[197] Here Jung wrote in the margin: substitute for life.

[198] Schmid is reasserting here his view that there is an introverted dimension to feeling (see 6 S, notes 132 and 135).

process." If we continue in this vein, simply countering statements by stating the opposite, without dealing with the other's arguments in more detail, we will finally end up in an unpleasant dispute about authority. Should it really come to this I would have to stress that despite my shorter analytical experience, when talking about the extravert, I as an extravert am more competent than you as an introvert to judge the nature of psychological processes in the extravert. Naturally, you are entitled to prove to me that I am erring about myself and the psychology of the extravert in general, and that I do not yet understand the processes in my own psyche. Your letter has not convinced me of this, however, although you know very well from experience that I have always been quite ready to be disabused of false views of myself.

Let me assume that in my last letter I did not succeed in expressing myself clearly enough, and let me try once again to explain my standpoint, even if repetitions cannot be avoided.

First of all, we should probably come to an agreement concerning the concept of *realization*, because I believe we have a completely different view of it. According to your letter, you seem to equate "realization" with "getting to know," or with "achieving knowledge," because in order to realize something you must put it outside yourself, objectify it, and can then achieve knowledge about it. I have used "realization" roughly in the sense the word is used, for instance, in the world of finance. To realize stocks means something like trying to find out how much value they represent, but not to sell them, convert them into money, quasi-objectify them.[199] So when I speak about the realization of a feeling, it means something like finding out about, or estimating, the value of this feeling. Here again value must not be mistaken for usefulness. In my experience, however, the value of a feeling cannot be experienced or estimated by thinking this feeling—as you claim—or even by "juxtaposing the feeling as an object, differentiating oneself

[199] Schmid is mistaken, however, because the German expression *realisieren*, like the English "to realize," means exactly that in this context: *in Geld umwandeln* = to turn into cash (*Duden*, Band 1, 21st ed., 1996).

from it," but, on the contrary, only by giving oneself completely over to a feeling, by surrendering to it, so that one is and feels "indistinguishable from the process." By thinking and objectifying the feeling, it gets instantly killed (the wind drops, as I wrote in my last letter). Its vitality, which is the essence of every feeling's value, turns into a lifeless phantom by being put outside oneself as a kind of self-subsisting entelechy.[200] One can certainly go on thinking about it, and thus perhaps recognize its usefulness, but one can never sense its real value in that way. Realizing feelings means really feeling, and not thinking, them. Perhaps the extravert must also have the courage at some point to be "an incurably extraverted dud"[201] in order to reach down into his own depths, and to realize and purify his feelings (assuming the eyes are a symbol of the intellect).

If I understand this correctly, a "compensated extravert" is for you somebody who has assimilated his thinking and his sensation, and has thus compensated his original, purely feeling type. Now what I wrote about the extravert in my last letter is exactly what does not apply to this compensated type. The latter has realized his thinking and sensation, and therefore has not needed to realize his feeling. My own understanding of the *ideally* oriented person corresponds completely to your explanation, but I differentiate between two kinds of the ideally oriented, those who are so in an archaic way, that is, whose feelings are unrefined, are undeveloped, coarse, and in an archaic state, and those equally ideally oriented ones who have refined and realized their feelings. But since this process of refinement and realization does not take the way of compensation, I cannot call these latter compensated. I think that we could equally differentiate between two kinds of ideally oriented introverts, those who think archaically and have not yet refined their thinking, and those who have in fact refined

[200] "In Aristotle's use: The realization or complete expression of some function; the condition in which a potentiality has become an actuality" (*The Oxford English Dictionary*, 1933 ed.). From Greek *enteles* (complete), *telos* (end, completion), and *echein* (to have).

[201] See 7 J.

it.[202] A person who has installed a motor in his boat is not someone whom we would call a good sailor, and a person who has affixed a sail to his boat, a motorboat expert. I distinguish between bad and good yachtsmen, between ideally oriented extraverts who are archaic and those who are not. Compensated extraverts are sailors with a built-in motor.

As I had the impression that, when speaking of introverts, you did not have those in mind who think in an archaic way, I took as a counterpart those extraverts who, although ideally oriented, no longer feel in an archaic way. What I tried to make very clear in my last letter, however, is that the refinement and realization of the extravert's feelings is *not* brought about by compensation. Therefore I must object to your statement that the realization of the extravert's feelings "proceeds from compensation, but not according to the principle of his type." The extravert refines his feelings solely according to the principle of his type; any attempt at compensation (i.e., at thinking and sensation) makes the realization of feelings impossible.

Let me try to juxtapose the solution you propose for the problem of the extravert with the same solution for the introvert.[203] If the *extravert* can purify his feelings only by achieving *knowledge* of them through *thinking*, the *introvert* would be able to purify his thinking only by an *evaluation* of his thoughts through *feeling*. You yourself write in your first letter, however, that you want to purify your thinking "of all pleasure and unpleasure caused by personal feeling."

I think, therefore, that the parallel process in both types is roughly the following: It is not by thinking about his feelings that the extravert realizes them—because thinking is a process heterogeneous to his nature that prevents a deepening [of his personality]—but, in following the view on the objective plane, by giving himself completely over to his feelings, to the point when he *feels* that he is violating both the object

[202] The rest of the passage, from here to the end of the paragraph, was written in the margin.

[203] Here a sentence is heavily struck out.

and also himself with his feelings.[204] Then comes the moment when he unites with his unconscious opposite (thinking and sensation)[205] in a natural way, not forced[206] by the object or its thinking, even if he has to "feel himself through" until he reaches the problem of double suicide, the *occide moriturus*.[207] Then he will also have to acknowledge that life is not the highest of goods. The parallel in the introvert I conceive as follows: it is not by feeling and evaluating his thoughts through feeling that the introvert realizes and refines his thinking—because feeling is a process heterogeneous to his nature that prevents the deepening of his personality—but, in following the view on the subjective plane, by giving himself completely over to his thoughts, to the point when he *knows* that he wants to force the object to come to him,[208] in order to satisfy his lust with it. Then comes the moment when he unites with his unconscious opposite (feeling and representation)[209] in a natural way, not forced by the feelings of the object, and when he would have to carry his thinking to the limit of madness. Then he will also see that knowledge is not the highest of goods. (I do not want to "lecture"[210] you on something with this sentence. I just imagine that you have repeatedly experienced something of the sort yourself, and know it better than I do, so that I am mentioning this only as a parallel.)[211]

[204] Here Jung made a big question mark in the margin.

[205] "opposite (thinking and sensation)" added later.

[206] Jung noted in the margin: why not forced?

[207] Latin for "kill and be slain," a reference to the love scene in Apuleius's *Metamorphoses, or The Golden Ass* (chap. 17), also quoted by Jung in 1911/12, § 610 (original p. 365), where it is linked to the notion of the eventual sacrifice of the libido, consuming both itself and its object.

[208] The rest of the sentence is added in the margin, instead of the struck out words: "and perhaps even finds pleasure himself in the process."

[209] Again representation is being seen as the fourth function beyond feeling, thinking, and sensation. Intuition had not yet been conceived as the name for this function (see 5 J and note 117, and introduction).

[210] Corrected from: "better."

[211] The following two paragraphs were written on a separate sheet of paper.

So I agree with you when you write that "the required exaggeration of the feeling makes the subject's lack of thinking and sensing activity *felt*." This is only the end result the extravert reaches, however. But we do not agree on *how* the extravert comes to this result. I know that I am referring to the dynamic aspect of the process with this, but I clearly emphasized in my last letter that we have different views about the *way* that leads to the purification of feeling. Insofar as this end result is not something that has to be achieved only once, having finally come to the end of the way, but must be achieved again and again, it seems to me that precisely the dynamic aspect—the progress in the development of the feelings, and the way toward it—is of the greatest importance.

With your statement that the extravert goes outward to the object, and not inward into the subject, you prove that I was right in my last letter to put forward the following proposition as the leitmotif of the introvert's misunderstandings of the extravert: it is inconceivable to the introvert that the extravert can find his own inner reality via feeling himself into the object, just as inconceivable as it is to the extravert that the introvert can adapt to the object via abstraction.

I have submitted to that famous extravert, as you call him, the remarks you made about him, and you might perhaps be interested in hearing what he had to say about them. He is grateful to the introvert *de pur sang*[212] for having allowed him complete freedom in his development, and for not having forced him, for example, to remain sitting in the saddle on which he had put him. He acknowledges that this effort is particularly deserving of thanks. He denies, however, that he was sitting in the saddle on which the introvert had put him when he galloped away to those adventures, as you put it. He maintains that he was not able to advance even one single step toward the realization of his feelings[213] so long as he remained sitting in this saddle, and felt compelled to abandon some,

[212] Schmid is of course talking about himself and Jung. See 7 J and note 154.
[213] "Toward the realization of his feelings" inserted later.

then more, and, finally, practically all views about relations with the object he had taken over from the introvert *de pur sang*, particularly the view on the subjective plane, which was an obstacle to the realization of his feelings. Only after he had discarded everything that had been between him and the horse was he able to "gallop away," and only then could he start to find a saddle that fitted his own and the horse's nature.

I would like to use the example of this same extravert to repeat a third assertion I made in the letter, which you oppose with a counterclaim. I claimed I was speaking of the extravert as he *is*, and not as he *ought to be*. You claim that after all I am indeed speaking of the extravert as he ought to be. Well, here I have to emphasize once again that, being an extravert myself, I surely should know how the extravert really is, and must therefore discuss a few more of your views on the extravert that in my experience do not correspond to reality.

Thus you write, among other things: "When the extravert finally understands the real nature of the object, he cools off considerably." As you know very well, one of the first tasks that this extravert had to solve was to see an object as it really is, or, as I usually call it, to separate the object from the ideal. Now I myself was surprised to see that the feelings of this extravert for the object in question did not cool off in the least through this process; they are as strong today as they were then when he galloped away on a bare horse.[214] (Although it is true that soon after solving this task that extravert had to change his attitude toward the object, this was because certain reactions of the object forced him to do so, but not because his feelings had cooled off by solving the above task.)[215]

I have since seen in other extraverts, too, that the feelings of a reasonably aesthetically receptive, sensitive extravert never cool off by his separating the ideal from the real object. As to why this is so, I would like to say only the following,

[214] Jung remarked in the margin: the object gets to feel it.

[215] The preceding sentence in parentheses was added at the bottom of the page.

although this question is of great importance for the psychology of the extravert: although the ideal that the extravert loves in the object does not correspond to the object as it is in reality or in the present, it more or less corresponds to the state toward which the object can, or could, develop out of the present stage. The extravert feels prospectively, as you yourself write, and in this prospective aspect lies perhaps one of the greatest life values of his feelings—but then, also the greatest danger. Separating the ideal from the person is not identical with the insight that the extravert loves an imago in the object, a symbolical value of one of his own tendencies. It is true that the feelings of the extravert cool off enormously during this procedure, which arises from the view on the subjective plane. They do not cool off, however, because the extravert realizes how the object really is, and that he *also* loved an ideal in the object. By the procedure of *recognizing* the imago, it can be demonstrated to an archaically feeling extravert that part of his feelings is egoistic (he loves only himself, his own tendencies, in the object). If this procedure is carried too far, however, every extravert will fight against this, and justifiably so, because love for the ideal in particular is not mere egoism. Admittedly, when the ideal and the object are separated, the ideal will correspond not *only* to the stage toward which the object develops. Part of the libido, which was originally directed also toward the object, will be used for the further development of an ideal, that is, if I may say so, for metapsychological processes. But these, too, will cause rather the opposite effect of a cooling-down.

Only an extravert who is ideally oriented in a completely archaic manner is "convinced from the outset that he has the other's best interest in mind, and that everything he does is beneficial for the other's well-being." The extravert easily makes this impression on the introvert, but he believes this as little as he believes that "his object is naturally delighted by getting his love." If he develops his capacity to feel himself into the other to only a minimal degree, he will *feel* that he can also do great harm to the other with his feelings, and, therefore, he will instinctively use his "virtue" with care. My experience teaches me that when the extravert locks up his feelings for another person who is either extraverted by constitution or in a phase of extraversion (e.g., in love with the extravert), in the crucible of abstraction, this other person will not experience this procedure as a violation, but will be stimulated by it to likewise bring his own still-undeveloped feelings to a boil in the crucible and thus realize his feelings.

I think the following parallel holds true for the introvert: in his relation with another introvert, the introvert will hardly have to fear that he causes harm with his abstract thinking, and thus will hardly have to care about using his "virtue" cautiously. Isn't the opposite true? The more the introvert makes his abstract thinking available to another introvert, the more the latter will be induced to purify his own thinking and to deepen his personality. I maintain that even in the following case it is worthwhile to take the object into consideration (here I am coming back to an example mentioned in the last letter): an extravert, "A," is loved by another extravert, "B." Now, when A assumes a compensated attitude toward B, that is, when he objectifies his feelings, and sees only a symbolical value in B, etc., I allege that B will feel outright violated by A's compensated attitude, albeit it in a passive[216] way. What B wants to get from A are not thoughts, but feelings, and the more abstract those are, the less he will feel violated. There also exists passive violation between people, and this passive violation is perhaps even harder to bear than an active one.

I believe, therefore, that only the respective opposite type will feel the abstraction process as a violation, since he is the only one for whom this "distillation runs counter to his nature." When an extravert believes he could find the deepening of his personality through a relation to an introvert *de pur sang*, he is like the man in your example who harnesses a horse to a railway train. It is only toward the introverted object that the extravert's feeling-into is not sufficient; in order

[216] Corrected from: negative.

really to see this object, he must realize also sensation and thinking. In other words, two different types, who are no longer preoccupied with the bare struggle for life, will understand each other only to the extent that they react to each other as compensated types and not as ideally oriented ones.

The extravert, too, does not imagine that he deepens the personality of the introvert by defending his standpoint of feeling. In assuming that the extravert wants, in his relation to the introvert, to "indoctrinate" and "better" the latter, you impute an intention to him, which he does not have even in the archaic, infantile state. The extravert does what he does not in order to achieve anything; he acts because he must act. Above all, he does not want to produce a particular effect, as you seem to believe. The view on the objective plane does not mean "wanting to better the other." It is not in the nature of the extravert to do something on purpose;[217] only if that were true would he really be violating the other. Whereas you accuse the extravert of wanting to dictate to the introvert how he would have to react to him, and allege that this is useless, since that's how the introvert *is* and that's how he has to react so as not to be devoured by the extravert, I believe I can with equal right accuse you of wanting to dictate to the extravert how he would have to react, and I must emphasize for my part that the extravert reacts just in the way I said. This happens and this is. The extravert is not a missionary but an instrument so designed by nature who must react as he does toward noncompensated introverts—not because of a missionary attitude, but simply because otherwise he would lose his wind in his relation toward the ideally oriented introvert.

Apparently, as your letters to me show, the introvert must also act in the same way in his relation to an extravert who defends the "ideal" attitude—namely, as an instrument, so to speak, although more passively, according to his nature.[218]

[217] Jung noted in the margin: ucs.

[218] The following sentence was added on a separate sheet of paper.

What you call mutual violation I consider an extremely ingenious arrangement of nature, only instead of the term "violation" I would use that of "interaction." After all, one cannot say that plants play the role of the missionary for the animal world because they produce the oxygen needed by the latter. These views notwithstanding, I am far from being a friend of eternal peace. When a people all too much develops what is its very own, however, its neighbor will wage war on it and will in turn develop its respective "own" in the process. Only by turning peace into war, and then establishing peace again, is development possible.

In many years of living together with an introvert, I have learned to adhere to the following maxim of a "Father," which you will probably allow me to quote, despite your reluctance to make use of such "arguments."[219] Lao Tzu ends his chapter 80 with the words:

> And when communities are so close to each other
> That the crowing of cocks and barking of dogs
> Can clearly be heard:
> *One should live, grow old, and die, but not unite.*[220]

For the communities to be able to live so close together without destroying each other, however, one thing seems to be necessary to me. Lao Tzu names it in the sixty-seventh chapter, as the first of the three treasures that he preserves and

[219] Cf. 7 J: "The words of the Fathers are a fine thing—so long as we do not use them as arguments."

[220] Lao Tzu, *Tao Te Ching*, "The Ideal Community (A Taoist Utopia)"; here translated directly from Schmid's German. Published translations into English offer a different meaning, for example: "The next place might be so near at hand that one could hear the cocks crowing in it, the dogs barking; but the people would grow old and die without ever having been there" (Waley, 1958, pp. 241–42). Gia-fu Feng and Jane English translate: "Though they live within sight of their neighbors, And crowing cocks and barking dogs are heard across the way, Yet they leave each other in peace while they grow old and die" (http://www.wussu.com/laotzu/laotzu80.html; 18 March 2011).

honors: the *feeling of reciprocity*. It "brings victory in war, and strength in peace."[221]

With best regards,
your Hans Schmid

P.S. I have the impression that I succeeded only very inadequately in describing what I feel to be my truth.[222] I hope your further reactions will allow me to give an ever-clearer picture of these problems, which are very difficult to grasp intellectually.

[221] Moss Roberts translates the Chinese word *ci*, for which Schmid offers "feeling of reciprocity," as "a mother's heart," because it "refers only to the love of a parent and a child—usually from the parental side" (Laozi, 2001, p. 166). In Red Pine, it is "compassion" (Lao-Tzu, 2009, p. 134). In Waley it is "pity," which "cannot fight without conquering or guard without saving" (1958, p. 225). In Gia-fu Feng and Jane English: "Mercy brings victory in battle and strength in defense. It is the means by which heaven saves and guards" (http://www.wussu.com/laotzu/laotzu80.html; 18 March 2011).

[222] Referring to Jung's statement that there are "two kinds of truth" (1 J).

9 J

THE LAST ONE[223]

6. Nov. 1915[224]

Dear Friend,

Your letter strengthens my conviction that reaching an agreement on the fundamental principles is impossible, because the point seems to be precisely that we do not agree. To this end the ucs. uses every means, and be it ever so hair-raisingly stupid. For instance, I have gone to the most stupid trouble to explain my viewpoint to you, while all the time you have been under a wrong impression in that you did not notice that that sentence in my first letter, in which I talked about the purification of thinking,[225] was purely hypothetical and referred *exclusively to the ideally oriented introvert*. It is on precisely this sentence that he is riding, right now, toward the perfection of his type, and thus into hell.

But in my last letter I consistently differentiated between the ideally oriented and the compensated types. So when you say that the introvert would have to *evaluate* his thinking by *feeling*, this is *precisely and absolutely correct*, and does in no way contradict what I said.[226] And, by the way, you have of course understood everything quite correctly, but suddenly your ucs. reminds you again of that misunderstood sentence and confuses everything anew. But this is a comedy, meant to prevent the feared union. This union, which should not come about, is the *union of the pairs of opposites in ourselves*. This

[223] I.e., (this is) the last letter.

[224] Date entered in different handwriting.

[225] Cf. 1 J: "I want to purge my thinking of all that is erratic and unaccountable, of all pleasure and unpleasure caused by personal feeling, and raise it to the height of justness and the crystal-clear purity of the universally valid idea, way beyond anything connected with mere feeling."

[226] Struck out: quite on the contrary.

is what the devil wants to prevent at any cost. *But it shall be nevertheless*. You constantly keep describing to me how the extravert achieves the perfection of his type. Well, I've known that for ages. What I am talking about, however, is how he can get out of his type. I have given you detailed arguments for why the process of realization is a process of gaining knowledge, and nothing else. You do not offer the slightest evidence that realization might be something different. On the contrary, your example of the realization of values shows that this is a process of *evaluation*. As already stated, it is only by underestimating the thinking process that you can conceive of evaluation as *doing*[227] and put the accent on it. But that's not where the accent should be.

It has long been a known fact that the extravert realizes his mistrust to a much too little extent. That's why I'm talking of it. As far as the last passage is concerned, well, reread your letter carefully—I haven't got it with me here—and you will understand my conclusion. That you had something else in mind I could not know.

It strikes me that, when speaking of knowledge, you always seem to have only the concept of "scientific" knowledge in mind. That is why I spoke of "living" knowledge as opposed to "scientific" knowledge. This distinction seems to have escaped you. If, as you think, life can be a substitute for this knowledge, we wouldn't need it. But then—how really stupid of life to create that knowledge which it does not need at all. In that case we need no longer bother about knowledge at all but simply go on living without racking our brains. You are again forgetting that life stands on two legs, *doing and*[228] *thinking*. So, if life can be a substitute for the Christian doctrine, what's the point of the doctrine? But how can I come to live a Christian life, if not through the doctrine? Even Christ taught, and did not simply live. If he had only lived, nobody would have noticed anything, or, if they noticed, they would not have understood.

[227] Doubly underlined.

[228] "and" doubly underlined.

If you feel like calling your thinking "feeling," you should tell me, for then I will also turn the thing around and call my feeling "thinking." You would be the first person to protest, because then I would simply foist my feelings on you, making them your thoughts. You would be flabbergasted by that, because then we would be right in the middle of a neurotic state of mind. If you conceive of your thinking as feeling, you will leave the door wide open for hysterical projections. Then talking is no longer possible. I have to remark, by the way, that there is at least one thing the introvert can do better than the extravert, and that is thinking. So one could well risk trying to give the introvert at least that much credit, namely, that his thinking could be more or less correct. You are right insofar as the process of realization is a feeling process in the extravert—well, certainly, so long as he is not compensated. We have just established, however, that we are now speaking of the compensated, and not of the "ideal," type. So long as even the realization process is a feeling process, there remains no room for thinking at all. And if the introvert mistakes even his feeling for thinking, well, what will become of his feeling?

There reigns a terrible confusion about the realization of thoughts and feelings. The extravert (the ideal type) must realize his feeling, the corresponding introvert his thinking. In this process, the extravert notices that his feeling is pregnant with thoughts; the introvert, that his thinking is full of feelings. I call the realization of thoughts hidden in feeling an act of thinking, and the realization of feelings hidden in thinking an act of feeling. Turning things around again only foolishly confuses matters and leads to nothing. Moreover, such a reversion leads to reversed results: for if I call my realizing act of feeling an act of thinking, I will again think my feelings as I did before, which is precisely the crazy thing to do, and the extravert will feel his thoughts, thus committing the same blunder as before. An introvert who does not outgrow his constant thinking is just as untenable as an extravert who cannot get out of his constant feeling. For starters, he must learn that thinking cannot be replaced at will by feeling, and that a thinking process cannot arbitrarily be seen as feeling. This is exactly the nonsense from which he suffers. For the ideal introvert, the purification of his thinking is, as already mentioned, precisely the indigestible morsel he is struggling with. His thinking has long since become refined enough, but the feelings therein are not yet realized; feelings can, in God's name, only be felt, but they can't—and that's the devil of it—ever be thought. It is true that it seems to him as if the realization of his feeling muddied and smudged his thinking, just as it seems to the extravert as if he killed his feelings. These evil things apply only to the hopelessly rationalistic slant in our thinking and feeling, however—in other words, to our so highly praised reason, into which we have advanced too far.

I won't say anything more about the "famous extravert," because I realize that all of a sudden he has now transferred onto the introvert what he had formerly claimed to have taken over from that other extravert.[229] Here one has to wait until matters have cleared up in him.

I believe you when you say that the feelings of the extravert are not cooled off by the knowledge of the object as it really is, but he himself cools off the object because, contrary to before, he treats it badly, and again disproportionately so. I do not give the object credit for cooling off, because for the object this is quasi unavoidable. For the object made the same mistake, by taking the other's fantasy at face value. Humans are close to one another only in the collective; in the individual sphere, they are separated by a huge distance, more so because they have to strive for separation and differentiation than because of being actually different.

That the introvert need not be careful with his thinking toward another introvert, but must, on the contrary, help him perfect his own thinking, is certainly true for the beginning of an analysis, provided the other introvert is not someone who has already carried his thinking to extremes (ideal type). Once the ideal type is reached, a quasi-total blocking of thinking takes place, which is lifted only momentarily when the intro-

[229] It is unclear who "that other extravert" is.

vert has realized a feeling. Vice versa, the same may be true for the extravert.

When I speak of the "intentions" of the extravert, I am well aware that it is just this that the extravert realizes to a much too little extent. He simply has these intentions (power tendency) in the ucs. And that is also why the extravert violates his object, for the ucs. takes effect. The more unconscious, the worse.

Regarding terminology, I must remark that the ideally oriented extravert is always archaic. He merely has differentiation on the one side, and archaism on the other, just like the introvert.

It is necessary to reach the ideal type. It seems we agree on that. Now the question is how to get out of it. This is possible only through self-communion, and this is true for both types, for both of them are too extraverted, because we are too extraverted in general.[230] This is the task of our time, which still has a monastery or desert of the soul in store for us. This is what is so damned bitter and difficult. Contact in the "human" and "civil" spheres, but anything to do with the "soul" cut off and kept ready for the development of individuality.[231] "Understanding" is a way toward a collective flattening of the individual and is discarded by fate.

It seems to me that scientifically it is possible to come to an understanding about the general principles of the types but not about the finer nuances. This is simply beyond what language can do. After all, everyone conceives of the linguistic signs for the various concepts in terms of what they have understood.

Now I would like to arrange the terms in question schematically:[232]

[230] Cf. 5 J, pp. 76–77, and note 116.

[231] Cf. Jung, 1911/12, §§ 258ff. (original pp. 180ff.), for Jung's thoughts on individuality versus individuation at the time.

[232] The following schema is full of corrections and insertions, which are not pointed out in detail here.

I. Introverted

CONSCIOUS

Thinking as the logical rational function (adapted and universally valid).

Feeling as tones of feelings subordinate to thinking, and as an emotional reaction to what had been cognized by thinking; *weak* as far as the outward effect is concerned.

UNCONSCIOUS

Feeling as a sporadic act of intuition[233] = a complex of *emotion*, with an *undeveloped* thought-content. Undeveloped, therefore archaic, symbolic, ambiguous, phenomenal, irrational, *actus purus naturae*,[234] can only imperfectly be formulated and grasped intellectually, *projected*.

II. Extraverted

CONSCIOUS

Feeling as the logical (logic of feeling) rational function[235] (adapted and universally valid).

Thinking as intellectual processes subordinate to feeling, and as a reaction to what had been felt (what had been comprehended by feeling). *Weak* as far as the outward effect is concerned.

Sensation, subordinate to feeling, a not very distinctive (or even disturbed) organ function.[236]

[233] On the introduction of intuition as a further "type" of conscious function by Moltzer in 1916, see "The Aftermath," pp. 29–30.

[234] Latin for a pure act of nature.

[235] See the introduction, pp. 24–25.

[236] See the introduction, p. 25.

UNCONSCIOUS

Thinking as a sporadic act of *intuition*[237] = a complex of *thoughts*, with an undeveloped content of feeling and sensation. The other attributes as above.

III.

The *general task* is the assimilation of the ucs.[238] The content of the ucs. contains dispositions

1. for outer life = concrete actions,
2. for inner life = subjective thinking and feeling.

IV.

Therefore, the *assimilation of the ucs.* is achieved by both

1. acting (experience via the object)[239] and
2. thinking, feeling as purely inner experience, or experience via the subject.

V.

It is *not determined a priori* what must be done in a concrete way, and what must be inwardly lived. This is *decided* by what is *possible* (subjectively and objectively).

[237] See the introduction, p. 24.

[238] MS: *Assimilierung des Ubw*. This is an early formulation of individuation, understood as development of the types of consciousness still in the unconscious.

[239] See the introduction, p. 25.

VI.

α. The ucs. content is *collective*, that is, subjective and objective, exopsychic and endopsychic, *irrational*, hence interfering with adaptation. (I.e., adaptation to the world and to the subjective condition, insofar as we have rationally cognized and felt it. *I am referring only to the analyzed person here.*)
β. The ucs. content is a unity of outer and inner meaning.
γ. It is not exclusively valid either (1) for the outer or (2) for the inner realm, but for both together, that is, for their *operating together*.

VII.

The ucs. content is *symbolic*, that is, encompassing the outside and the inside, because the symbol is (1) an *act*, but not in the sense of an act pure and simple, and (2) a *thought*, but not in the sense of a rational concept.

VIII.

The symbol is thought and act combined into a unity, collectively and individually, socially and egoistically.

IX.

The general analytical task is accomplished by the assimilation of the ucs. content. Therefore the ucs. content is the *object at which the analytically educated libido aims*. (The way of education is via the object and the subject.)

X.

The general object at which the libido aims has the significance of a *cultural ideal*. It is the dearest and the highest (the treasure hard to obtain), hence a *religious* goal, thus hinting at bringing together all the strongest strivings.

XI.

Company of like types eases things, and holds fast to what is already given, thus serving the extension and consolidation of what had been taken [from the other]. Balance and understanding are possible, desirable, and absolutely to be strived for. (Being.)

XII.

Company of unlike types complicates things, as it is an obstacle, and for that very reason an absolute necessity of development, hence also a temptation to regression. He who does not win in this process, loses. Balance and understanding are impossible, neither desirable nor to be strived for. The disparity can be obscured only by deceit and violence. The only thing in common is the goal. (Becoming.)[240]

In the meantime, and after long deliberation, the problem of resistance against *understanding and coming to an agreement*[241] has become clear to me. It was Birgitta of Sweden (1302–73) who helped me to gain that insight.[242] She saw the

[240] Here, in the middle of the seventh handwritten page, this section of the letter ends. The rest of the letter starts on a fresh page, and is written with a different pen. See also note 247.

[241] In the original: *Verständigung*, which has both these connotations.

[242] Birgitta Birgersdotter (1302/3–73), daughter to an influential Swedish aristocratic family. After the death of her husband in 1345, she had visionary experiences that concerned her plans to found a religious order, or in which

devil in a vision; he spoke to God, and said the following about the psychology of devils: "*Her belly is so swollen, because her greed was boundless*, for she filled herself and was not sated, and so great was her greed that, had she been able to gain the whole world for herself, she would gladly have made the effort and, moreover, would have liked to reign also in the heavens. I have the same greed. Could I win all the souls in heaven and earth and in the purgatory, I would gladly capture them."

So the devil is the devourer. To understand = *comprendere* = *katasyllambanein*,[243] and also to devour. Understanding and agreement are an act of swallowing. One should not let oneself be swallowed, however, unless one is really someone who can overpower the monster from within. Provided, too, that the other accepts the role of Fafnir[244] and devours indigestible heroes. So it is better not to "understand" people who might be heroes, because this will not agree at all with oneself. One can go under through them. In the wish to understand, which seems to be so ethical and all human, there lurks a devil's will, which, though I myself may not notice it at first, definitely makes itself felt to the other. Understanding is a terribly binding power, possibly a veritable soul murder when it levels out vitally important differences. The core of the individual is a mystery of life, which dies when it is "grasped." That is also why *symbols want to keep their secrets*; they are mysterious not only because we are unable to clearly see what is at their bottom. For the symbol wants to prevent Freudian interpreta-

---

Christ and/or Mary told her to relay messages to others, often about the necessary reform of the church through the reform of religious and secular rulers. After her death, hundreds of her visions were edited and published in Latin, and her writings were much copied and translated throughout the1400s. A biography and links to works available online at http://home.infionline.net/~ddisse/birgitta.html (18 March 2011).

[243] Greek, *kata* = down, downward; *syllambanein* = to take or gather together, to grasp.

[244] A figure in Norse mythology. He and his brother Regin killed their father to get the latter's gold treasure. Fáfnir decided he wanted it all, turning into a dragon who guarded the treasure. Regin then sent Sigurd to kill the dragon. Sigurd succeeded, thus winning the treasure himself.

tions, which are indeed so pseudo-correct that they never fail to have an effect. For ill people, "analytical" understanding is as healingly destructive as cauterization or thermocautery, but healthy tissue is banefully destroyed by it. After all, it is a technique we learned from the devil, always destructive, but useful where destruction is necessary. We can commit no greater error, however, than to apply the principles of this technique to an analyzed psychology.

But there's still more to this! All understanding as such, being an integration into general viewpoints, contains the devil's element, and kills. It tears another life out from its own peculiar course, and forces it into something foreign in which it cannot live. That is why, in the later stages of analysis, we must help the other to come to those hidden and unopenable symbols, in which the seed of life lies securely hidden like the tender seed in the hard shell. Actually, there must not be any understanding and agreement on this, even if it were possible, as it were. But if understanding and agreement on this have become generally and obviously possible, the symbol is then ripe for destruction, because it no longer covers the seed, which is about to outgrow the shell. Now I understand a dream I once had, and which greatly impressed me: I was standing in my garden, and I had dug open a rich spring of water, which gushed forth mightily. Then I had to dig a trench and a deep hole, in which I collected all the water and let it flow back into the depths of the earth again. In this way salvation is given to us in the unopenable and unsayable symbol,[245] for it protects us by preventing the devil from swallowing the seed of life. The threatening and dangerous thing about analysis is that the individual appears to be understood: the devil takes away and eats up his soul, which had been born into the light as a naked and exposed child, robbed of its protective cover. This is the dragon, the murder, which always threatens the newborn Son of God. He must be hidden once again from the "understanding" of men.

[245] In the second layer of *Liber Novus*, written sometime in 1915, Jung articulated a new valorization of the symbol (cf. Jung, 2009, pp. 310f.).

True understanding, however, seems to be what is not understood, yet still is and is effective. When Ludwig the Saint once visited St. Giles incognito, and when the two, who did not know each other, caught sight of each other, they both fell to their knees before the other, and embraced and kissed—but *did not talk*.[246] Their gods knew each other, and their humanness followed. We must understand the divine within us, but not the other, insofar as he is able to go and stand on his own. We have to understand the ill person, however, for he is in need of the cauterizing remedy. We should bless our blindness for the other's mysteries, because it prevents us from devilish deeds of violence. We should be confidants of our own mysteries, but chastely veil our eyes before the mysteries of the other, insofar as he does not need "understanding" because of his own incapability.[247]

[246] A story told in *The Little Flowers of Saint Francis of Assisi* (1340; English edition 1905), the most popular biography of St. Francis, written by an anonymous Italian friar: Ludwig of Thuringia (1214–70), king of France, having heard of the sanctity of Brother Giles (in German: Aegidius), one of the first companions of St. Francis, went to meet him. They had never met before in their lives, but knelt down and embraced each other, without speaking a word. When asked why he had not spoken to the King, St. Giles answered that nothing had needed to be said because "the light of divine wisdom revealed his heart to me and mine to him" (ibid., p. 111).

[247] The extant letter ends here (in the middle of the page) without greetings.

10 S[248]

Solothurn, 1–7 Dec. 15

Dear Friend,

As you do not wish any further discussion, I will not deal with the first six pages of your letter, nor with some views expressed in your accompanying letter,[249] which seem debatable to me.

Your explanation of the resistance against understanding is very good in my opinion. It is my impression that the first step toward appreciation of the extravert is made by no longer wanting to understand him. I believe that the most important problems of the extravert cannot be grasped intellectually at all, just as the most important problems of the introvert cannot be grasped by feeling. I can imagine that it is as difficult to appreciate a problem by way of feeling, without wanting to understand it intellectually, as it is difficult—according to my experience with introverts—to understand something intellectually, without wanting to accept it with our feelings. I learned this by realizing that I have to accept as facts the problems of the introvert, which can be understood only intellectually.

Just as the introvert must see that there is "also" the devil lurking behind his wish to understand, the extravert must see that there is "also" the devil lurking behind his compulsion of feeling himself into the other. (For the extravert, understanding means "feeling into.")

[248] The extant correspondence ends with this and the following three letters from Schmid. Transcription and translation of all four letters are based on photocopies kindly made available by Hans Schmid's grandson, Florian Boller, through the mediation of Ulrich Hoerni of the Stiftung der Werke von C. G. Jung. No further letters from Jung have been found at this time.

[249] Schmid probably refers to the two parts of the previous letter, that is, Jung's exposure of his general views and his outline of introversion/extraversion and the functional types, which occupy the first six and a half pages of the previous letter, on the one hand, and the following passage on Birgitta of Sweden and the dangers of "understanding," on the other (see note 242).

Although I agree with you on this, it still seems to me that the psychology of the extravert can be explained to a still greater extent, also intellectually,[250] than has been done in our correspondence so far. As you can see from the postscript to my last letter, I regret that you broke off this correspondence. I still had a few things to say about how in the course of time I learned to understand, purely intellectually, myself and other extraverts. But perhaps the introvert can reach this understanding of the extravert only after no longer wishing to understand him.

In reading the two last, very interesting and generous pages of your letter, it became clear to me that my assumptions when beginning this correspondence were completely different from yours. It was never my intention and wish to understand you or the psychology of the introvert through it, or even to feel myself into you. As you know, this correspondence grew out of another, smaller exchange of letters, which itself grew out of our oral discussions that have lately become more and more heated.[251] I was forced to the latter two[252] by the *feeling* that you did not appreciate something in the extraverted character, and the most valuable in it to boot, less so in purely intellectual discussions, but more in the feeling sphere, as shown by your reactions. I found myself compelled, therefore, to defend my point of view against you. I concede that I made the mistake, particularly in our oral discussions, of demanding all too much that I be accepted. This was due to my inferiority feelings, to my too weak belief in what I would like to call, in short, my truth. Today I know that, if my truth is truth, it will remain my truth, even if you cannot accept it.

The longer our correspondence went on, the more I became convinced that this feeling, which at the time drove me to enter into those heated discussions, was correct. Thus it was not in order to instruct you, or to play the role of the Savior for you, that I tried to show you the extravert as I understand

[250] "also intellectually" inserted later.

[251] No such "smaller exchange of letters" has been found so far. See letter 11 S, in which Schmid quotes from previous correspondence.

[252] That is, 6 S and 8 S.

him, but out of an instinct of self-preservation. The necessity to be accepted is not identical with the wish to be understood. It is perfectly possible to work together on the same project with someone else without being completely[253] understood by the other, but it is impossible without being accepted as a fact, and this also in the feeling sphere.[254] I know that you have done what you could, vis-à-vis the extravert and myself, to accept him. It is not my task to search for the outer and inner reasons that prevented you from advancing further in this. I also know very well that much has still to be "cleared up" in that "famous extravert," but I cannot believe that the one type is only then able to accept the functions of the other when these have been "cleared." This would be in contradiction to all laws of development.

I fully agree with you that the healthiness of the project on which we both work depends on the difference of the functions. This differentiation must not be carried too far, however, so that the heart, for example, rejects the blood coming from the liver as unpurified or unnecessary. Only that organism lives healthily, after all, in which all the different functions of the organs work together harmoniously. My understanding of Lao Tzu's *feeling* of reciprocity is that it enables the working together of completely differentiated organs. And this must result, in my opinion, in a certain harmony. (Harmony is based on the consonance of two *differentiated* tones.) This harmony may be found only in the symbol, however. Only the symbol can, of the two opposed standpoints of truth and beauty, be beautiful and true at the same time.

Now I also understand why it was impossible for me until now to tell you something about what has been the most important work to me during the last months.[255] Its topic is probably about the same as what you call, so rightly and beautifully,

[253] One word heavily struck out.

[254] The rest of this passage, from here to the end of the paragraph, was added at the bottom of the next page.

[255] Iselin (1982, p. 149) surmises that this probably refers to Schmid's book, *Tag und Nacht* (*Day and Night*), which seems quite unlikely, however, since the book did not appear until 1931. This rather seems to be a reference to the

the "mystery of life." With the help of the black book and the dreams,[256] I came to unexpected insights about the "core of individuality." As far as I can see, the compacted formulas, the symbols of the mystery, are the same for both types, but the ways leading to it are opposed to each other. So far it was my impression that your attitude, which "wishes to understand," could not accept my ways; so I kept silent.

I, too, bless my blindness for the other's secrets, but I still have the feeling that—provided the introvert no longer wants to understand, and the extravert no longer wants to feel himself into the other—both are able, if not to understand each other, then to accept each other in formulas of thinking and feeling, and this to a greater extent than has been the case between the two of us so far.

Now as to our correspondence, my view is the following: it has long been clear to me that it can never be published in this form. I would like to leave open the question, however, whether it would not be a very good thing to create a certain confusion by making it available to a smaller circle. Perhaps this would counteract a certain one-sidedness into which, in my opinion, we have gotten over time. But we would both have to adopt what you describe as the "superior standpoint" toward the correspondence. I will answer to the work, which you are now preparing for the society,[257] by formulating a counterposition, which I would read *before* your paper will be discussed. I would not like to start on a work of my own right now, because we would run the risk of talking at cross-purposes. I do have the impression, however, that this will lead

---

fact that "Hans Schmid also wrote and painted his fantasies in something akin to *Liber Novus*" (Shamdasani, 2009, p. 204; see the following note).

[256]Unclear. On Jung's so-called black book(s), see Shamdasani's introduction in Jung, 2009. It is possible that Schmid refers to one of those, which Jung had let him read, and to dreams of Jung recorded therein, but much more likely that he refers to the similar project of his own and his own dreams.

[257]MS: *Verein*. The reference is to the Verein für analytische Psychologie (Society for Analytical Psychology), where Jung gave a presentation on "historical contributions to the type question" on 3 June 1916 (*Protokolle* etc.). The minutes do not mention a contribution of Schmid.

to the same confusion as making the correspondence available. For my part, I would have preferred to discuss, or rather continue, it beforehand, and only then to work further on the problems contained therein.

Perhaps we must, for the time being, work it out between ourselves on a different basis in order to achieve a truly superior standpoint, before presenting it to others.

With best regards,
Hans Schmid

11 S

Basel, 11–14. XII. 15

Dear Friend,

In order to write you openly and honestly, I have to overcome certain intellectual resistances, for I know from experience that it is nearly impossible for the introvert to acknowledge important problems, if life does not force him to gain knowledge. So, although I do not fancy that my answer will be able to tell you anything, I want to follow your invitation as best I can.[258]

I understand very well why extraverts have so far offered you only vague allusions to what you should not [*sic*] acknowledge. It is nearly impossible to talk about this intellectually, because this is about things that can be fully grasped only by feeling, never by the intellect. If for you clearness means that a problem is described intellectually in a clear way, you demand the impossible from me in wishing that I "clear the air" in such a way.

I want to come back to the, admittedly unclear, allusion I made in my last letter: I spoke of my feeling that you cannot appreciate something in the extraverted character, and the most valuable in it to boot.

The most valuable trait of the extravert must lie in the qualities of his feeling, and I would say that the most valuable among them is his capacity for love. In my opinion, this constitutes the core of his individuality; it contains his "divinity." As a matter of fact, however, this core contains not only a high, divine, and beautiful love but also a low, devilish, and ugly love.

I do not want to write an apotheosis of love. For me Plato's works, especially the connection he makes between the Eros

[258] As becomes clear from the concluding sentence in this letter, Jung had invited Schmid to write "openly and honestly" about his thoughts, even if he, Jung, had already wanted to bring the correspondence to a formal end in 9 J.

and the beautiful, are such an apotheosis. Other examples can be found in the Bible.

When I read your letter, the first thing that came to mind was a motto (!) for my answer, and I do not want to withhold it from you: "Nevertheless I have somewhat against thee, because thou hast left thy first love" (Revelation 2:4).[259]

So let me expand on my vague allusion by saying that I have the feeling that you do not, in your feeling, accept the power of Eros—as Plato understood it—and the greatness of love—as Christ (but not the apostles, or contemporary Christians) taught it—to the extent it must be accepted (for the path taken by the mechanism of the sublimation of feelings is via these concepts, via the symbol of devoted love and sympathy, while the path taken by the respective mechanism of the sublimation of thinking is via the symbol of sacrifice).

Now you will demand that I supply evidence for the correctness of this feeling. I could gather evidence from three different areas:

1) From your own works. The problem of love is hardly mentioned in your work on the libido, for example. Spontaneous love is something infantile. Love seems to be understandable only as a manifestation of the pleasure-unpleasure principle. Love is playing the savior or the missionary, etc., etc. For the moment I do not want to enter into these proofs in more detail. The critical part of my work on Tristan[260] will deal with that.
2) From what I observed in your reactions to other people close to you. I will, God forbid!, never produce this evidence; because it is up to those people, once they have developed into independent individuals, who also acknowledge their feelings, to react to your reactions, and not up to me to criticize the latter.
3) The only area I want to deal with in more detail here are your reactions toward me.

[259] Spoken by Christ to the congregation in Ephesus. Quoted in ancient Greek in the original; rendered here in the King James version.

[260] See note 162.

You write that you acknowledge the difference between my and your way of thinking and feeling. I have indeed nice pieces of evidence for this. In acknowledging their difference, you acknowledge their existence but not necessarily the *value* (not: usefulness) of the extravert's thinking and feeling. Under point 3 you write that you acknowledge my intellectual and *moral* capabilities. Why do you speak of "moral," and not, in parallel to point 2, of thinking and *feeling* capabilities? I can't imagine that you acknowledge the feeling of the extravert only if it is moral. What do you understand by moral? Couldn't that, which is moral to the introvert, be immoral to the extravert, and vice versa?

That you do not acknowledge the extravert's capacity for love, indeed often debase it, is shown to me by many passages in our correspondence. I do not want to repeat them bit by bit. Should you reread your letters sometime from a superior standpoint, you will probably notice yourself the strangely affective, often downright ironic-spiteful tone with which you speak of the love of the extravert. I am convinced that any reader with a modicum of impartiality will get the impression from our correspondence up to now that you do not do justice to the psychology of the extravert in it.

On 4 June 1915, you wrote me: "I do not even know your products, because you did not yield any of them."[261] To which I answered: "Obviously you can acknowledge only very specific products of mine, namely, only intellectual ones," and I went on saying that my most valuable products will never be intellectual ones. Our correspondence has shown me once again that to this day you have been unable to acknowledge with your feeling the extravert's feeling capacity, his sympathy, his love, and his friendship.

I see further proof of this in the following reaction of yours: On 6 June I tried to explain to you what I mean by friendship. On 9 June you turned the tables back on myself with the words: "You should rather have a look at the resistances against me,

[261]This phrase and the following quotes from previous correspondence cannot be found in the extant letters.

of which you are full." To this day I have been unable to find those resistances. I hardly believe one can speak of resistances when someone does not share the other's opinion.

I can imagine that my feeling, "you do not acknowledge with your feeling what is valuable in the extravert," still today impresses you as a "fantasy wandering off into the blue," and that you will have resistances against this fantasy now as you had then.

No letter can clearly prove to you what I feel about your nonacknowledgement; this can be done, in my view, only by the knowledge you yourself gain by experiencing.

Nonetheless, I wrote you openly and honestly what I think, because you wanted it.

With best regards,
Hans Schmid

I will return home on Tuesday evening.

12 S

Basel, 17/18. XII. 15.

Dear Friend,

I was not surprised by your reaction to my honest letter.[262] As you sent it to Solothurn, despite my postscript, it arrived only this evening. I have now *thought* it through and have come to the conclusion that it is a prime specimen of Mephistophelean wisdom. Its end provoked a laughter of relief, for which I heartily thank you.

Too bad that these truths are nothing new to me. I have an equally sharp-tongued Mephistopheles within myself, who already showed me the same truths about God and the Devil, Eros and the Poisoner,[263] etc., in an even more drastic manner long ago, particularly in the black book.[264]

I need no longer to *demand* the acknowledgement of the value of my love, neither from you nor from other people. I acknowledge its worth as well as its worthlessness. So I do not demand anything from you that I'm not doing myself.

Moreover, I did not demand anything from you at all; I simply did what you asked and told you of a feeling I have toward you, a feeling that is proved right to me again and again, and particularly also by your present reaction. My motive for leading this correspondence was not only *my* being acknowledged by you but the feeling that it is not yet possible for you to acknowledge an important, divine as well as devilish, power of the inner life of all humans, and because I was worried about the effects of your one-sidedness on our work.

[262] Missing; see 10 S, note 248.

[263] An allusion to Plato's *Symposium*, in which Socrates relates what Diotima had taught him about Eros/Love: an intermediate being between wisdom and folly, beyond good and evil, sometimes blossoming, sometimes dying, intermediate between the divine and the mortal, a sorcerer and a poisoner.

[264] Again, probably a reference to his own "black book."

If I also fought for being acknowledged myself, this was out of an instinct of self-preservation, because I, like any other honest extravert, cannot collaborate in a work that does not take my divine and devilish parts into account. But this does not mean that I demanded anything from you. I can well go my way alone. Yet I still believe that analysis will be able to prevent another splitting.[265]

Acknowledgement or acceptance does not mean *blind* acceptance, or even adoration, to me, by the way, even though the intellect has to be dimmed so that the power that lies in the realm of feelings can be acknowledged. It seems to me, however, that a power can also be acknowledged when its one side is devilish.

Nevertheless I know that I have always acknowledged, and will always acknowledge, in private and in public, in speech and in writing, the value of your thoughts; actually I also accepted your untruths at first, that is, also your devil. This was the only way it was possible for me to really acknowledge you. I cannot understand why you distinguish so painstakingly between moral and immoral, between divine and devilish love, in the extravert. They simply cannot be separated, because out of both—just as out of truth and untruth—the new develops again and again.

Nor do I demand that you feel in the way I want you to. This reproach has been beaten to death, and no longer applies.[266] I well nigh know the kind of feelings of the introvert, but vis-à-vis a nearly complete lack of feeling-into I am feeling as much as a fish in the air as an introvert toward an extravert who cannot think at all.

I cannot grant that it belongs to the *typical* standpoint of the one type to treat the other ironically, or even to debase him, and that someone who does not do this will have to adopt the *superior* standpoint.

[265] Possibly not a reference to a splitting between the two of them but to another splitting in the analytic movement, like Jung's from Freud, this time in the Zurich school.

[266] Original: *trifft nicht mehr*, which can mean both "no longer applies" and "no longer hurts."

Incidentally, I already wrote in my last letter that I do not believe that letters will convince you of the correctness of my feeling, which is also shared by others. As mentioned, this can be done only by knowledge gained from experience, provided one still concedes that experience can have some influence on one's knowledge at all.

To conclude, I would juxtapose your "wonderful" Viennese idyll[267] with a "bitterly true" idyll on Lake Zurich.

There you are, sitting in a tower on the *Obersee*,[268] having become Nietzsche's heir, father to none, friend to none, and sufficient unto yourself. Vis-à-vis, here and there, a few other male and female introverts are living, each in their tower, loving humankind in those "farthest away," thus protecting themselves against the devilish love of their closest "neighbors." And, from time to time, they meet in the middle of the lake, each in their motorboat, and prove to each other the dignity of man.

With best regards,
Hans Schmid

[267]Unclear reference; to a statement in Jung's missing letter?

[268]This creates a further mystery: Schmid's letter is clearly dated 17/18 December 1915, in his own handwriting, and contextually it does follow up on 11 S, where Schmid admitted he wanted to write "honestly," and 12 S, where he refers to Jung's reaction to his honest letter. However, the reference to a tower on the *Obersee* (upper lake), where Jung did eventually build his tower in Bollingen in 1923, is enigmatic. Perhaps Jung had already told him about such a plan or fantasy in his missing letter, or on one of their joint sailing trips, during which "a wish must have grown in them to build a refuge with simple means in natural surroundings" (Iselin, 1982, p. 19) or Schmid's remark is uncannily premonitory.

13 S

Basel, 6. I. 16.

Dear Friend,

The days spent in the Ticino have had a double effect on me; they clarified my views on the relation between the two types and were confusing with regard to the solution of my own core problems. I no longer find this confusion bothersome as I used to, however, but stimulating, and I hope that we will more and more succeed in having a sort of contact, which confuses only inasmuch as it is beneficial.

I am still occupied with the problem of matter and form, and I cannot settle for the formulation we found.[269] Referring to the circles made by the waves in the lake, I said: I can find the form only in and by myself, and nobody must disturb my circles in the process; but the form I find only through the intersection between my circles and those of others. You replied that things were the other way around for you, that for you the form came from within, while others provided the matter for it. That's what I still remember.

I would like to develop that thought further: The introvert, too, provides the matter, namely, his thoughts, but as thoughts they are formless. Once you told me that it repeatedly struck you how your secretary Moltzer[270] rendered thoughts that you had told her in a more acceptable and lively form. So perhaps the extravert has the capability of clearly formulating thoughts, and the introvert provides the matter in the form of

[269] No sources for such a discussion could be found.

[270] On Moltzer, see note 87. She "worked closely with Jung as his assistant" (Shamdasani, 1998a, p. 57). In 1915 Jung confirmed to Jelliffe that he "trusted ... cases entirely to her with the only condition, that in cases of difficulties she would consult me.... Later on Miss M. worked quite independently" (ibid.). As to her role as Jung's "secretary," she occasionally attended to his correspondence while he was away (letter from Moltzer to Freud, 24 April 1912; Freud Archives, University of Essex).

his thoughts. Vice versa, the extravert provides matter in the form of his feelings, while they are given form by the introvert. The extravert finds the form only through the intersection with other circles.

The extravert projects his incapability of finding a form for his feelings into the introvert, and that is why he always wants to correct the introvert's feelings. Perhaps the introvert, too, inasmuch as he wants to correct at all, has the analogous tendency to correct the form of the thoughts of the extravert.

Insofar as everybody possesses both tendencies, in my case only those of my feelings have a form, which have been formed by the thinking process, and only those thoughts appear formed to me, which have been approved by my feeling.

I would be interested in hearing your thoughts about this.

Marthe[271] and I are in a salutary state of war.

With best regards,
Hans Schmid

[271] His wife, Marthe Schmid-Guisan.

Appendix

Summary of Jung's First Three Letters

Editors' note: This summary is quite obviously from Jung's own hand, presumably written when considering the correspondence for publication. The translation is based upon the text as published by Iselin (1982, pp. 122–30).

Types

Jung: Correspondence with Schmid

1.

A person with intellectual abilities instinctively prefers to adjust to the object by way of thinking (abstraction), whereas a person whose feeling exceeds his intellectual abilities prefers to adjust to the object by way of feeling himself into it. This results in the rational quality of thinking in the former and the rational quality of feeling in the latter. Owing to the preference of thinking, feeling-into will remain in a relatively undeveloped state and will thus function in an irregular, unpredictable, and uncontrollable way—in one word, irrationally. Naturally man, ever mindful of his role as *Homo sapiens*, tries to control the irrational with the rational, so that the thinking person wants to force his feeling to serve his thinking, and the feeling person his thinking to serve his feeling.

The stronger my ideal is, and the more I cherish it, the more I actually have to condemn the other, because he[272] acts contrary to my ideal—which I naturally consider to be *the* ideal. After all, I want to purge my thinking of all that is erratic and unaccountable, of all pleasure and unpleasure of personal

[272] In Iselin: *es* = it. Very probably either a writing error of Jung's, or an error in the transcription, for *er* = he (see the almost identical passage in 1 J).

feeling, and raise it to the height of justness and the crystal-clear purity of the universally valid idea, way beyond anything connected with mere feeling. You, on the contrary, want to put your feeling above your personal thinking and to free it from all the fantasized and infantile thoughts that might impede its development. That is why the thinking person represses his all-embracing feeling, and the feeling person his all-embracing thinking. But the thinking person accepts feelings that correspond to his thinking, and the feeling person accepts thoughts that correspond to his feeling.

I even suspect that the thinking person speaks of feeling when he is actually thinking, and the feeling person of thinking when he is feeling. It is certain, however, that what the feeling person calls thinking is just a *representation* but not an abstraction. His approach to thinking is therefore extraordinarily concretistic, and it is immediately noticeable that it cannot turn into an abstraction. Vice versa, the feeling of the thinking person is not at all what the feeling person would call feeling, but is really a *sensation*, as a rule of a reactive nature, and thus very concretistic, if not to say "physiological."

3.

The introvert does not comprehend the object directly but by means of abstraction, that is, by a thinking process that is inserted between himself and the object. The attitude he assumes toward the object is a certain *rejection*, therefore, which can even grow into a kind of fear of the object. His primary reaction toward the object is actually not love, but rather fear. It is likely that in the unconscious of the introvert there is a love for the object that compensates his fear of it, while in the unconscious of the extravert there is a fear that compensates his love for the object. In pathological cases, unconscious love also becomes a source of heightened fear of the object for the introvert, and, conversely, unconscious fear becomes a source of powerful attraction to the object for the extravert.

It is not so that the thinking person is quasi-characterized by the absence of feeling, and the feeling person by the absence of thinking, which would certainly be completely wrong.

The introvert does feel, too, and very intensely so, only in a way different from the extravert.

This *hypothetical thinking*—which is by no means the expression of a personal opinion—is extraordinarily misleading for the extravert, because he is always inclined to understand such an expression in a concrete way. Conversely, the introvert is always led by the nose by the extravert's hypothetical feeling.

The introvert needs the object for his thinking, because it is precisely via the object that he adapts to outer reality. I'd like to say that this is exactly where his mistake lies: *he thinks objects*, instead of feeling them, for these objects are, after all, human beings who quite refuse to be only thought, although the introvert fancies that he is actually loving the object in this way.

The introvert cannot follow the other's *hypothetical feeling*, which feels like a loveless experiment to him. He feels it in this way because he feels concretistically, whereas the extravert can *feel abstractly* beyond the object, just like the introvert can *think abstractly* beyond the object, which naturally is felt as equally loveless by the extravert.

The introvert, too, loves the object, through his thinking; indeed, it is indispensable for his thinking. This is not so for the extravert. For him, the object is an obstacle for his thinking, because his thinking disregards the object. The *representation of the extravert* refers completely to the object, and is, therefore, in complete agreement with *outer reality*, while his thinking is in agreement with his own *inner reality*. This is not the case in the introvert. His representation of things is inadequate, precisely because of the lack of feeling-into [the object]. His thinking is in accordance with outer reality, however, but not with his own inner reality. This explains that the introvert thinks and preaches all sorts of nice things, but does not do them himself, in fact, but does the contrary; whereas the extravert does all sorts of good and nice things, but does not think them, but the contrary. The extravert has flourishing social contacts, the introvert does not. The extravert knows, by feeling himself into others, by what human means people can be won over, whereas the introvert tries to create values in himself with which he tries to impress and force others toward him or even bring them to his knees. He does this with the help of the power principle, while the extravert does it with the pleasure-unpleasure mechanism.

The more ideal the attitude of a type is, the more likely his plan will fail. For if I develop an ideal attitude I will become one-sided. If I am one-sided, however, I will stretch the pairs of opposites in my nature apart, thus activating the unconscious standpoint that runs directly counter to my own ideal.

Thus it comes that the extravert, with his idealistic attitude, gathers inferior followers around him who, although they seem to be faithfully and gratefully devoted to him, actually flatter his unconscious power principle in Byzantine ways. Independent persons turn away from him, however—ungratefully, as he says—which naturally makes him feel misunderstood in his most ideal values.

The ideally oriented introverted person is faced with the fact that he scares away from himself precisely the human love and joy that he is really trying to find behind all his desire to impress and to be superior, and thus he keeps and chains to himself only those inferior persons who know best how to cater to his desire. This explains, for instance, the well-known fixation of introverted scholars or other intellectually superior persons to women of an inferior type, to whores and the like. The fault lies in straining the ideal attitude too much.

Now the solution of this problem is intimately connected with the *interpretation on the subjective plane*. The only goal for the ideally oriented introvert is the *production of impersonal, imperative values*, and for the equally ideally oriented extravert the only goal is the *love for the object. But both these endeavors are of a hypothetical nature, however*. They do not express man's true nature but are mere hypotheses about how the desired goal might be reached. While the introvert's conscious attitude is an impersonal and just attitude of power, his unconscious attitude aims at inferior lust and pleasure; and while the extravert's conscious attitude is a personal love for human beings, his unconscious attitude aims at unjust, tyrannical power.

The interpretation on the subjective plane is trying to mediate between the two. *Its aim is to help the individual accept his unconscious opposite.*

The introvert also tries, through the hypothesis of abstraction, to reach the object, actually reality, which seems to him chaotic only because of the projection of his unused and therefore undeveloped feeling. He tries to conquer the object by thinking. But he wants to reach the object quite as much as the extravert. The extravert wants to get to the object but actually only in order to come to himself by going beyond it. He has fled from himself, because his unused and, therefore, chaotic world of thoughts has made it unpleasant, even unendurable, for him to stay with himself.

Because of the nonacceptance of the unconscious opposite, the typical ideal striving leads to a disastrous violation of the other, and the worst thing is that neither of them notices why he is violating the other.

5.

I have to admire the extravert's capacity to move ahead of the difficulty, and beyond it, with his feeling. The extravert feels prospectively, the introvert retrospectively, so that the latter remains longer under the impression of the difficulty.

For me it is essential that both, the rational as well as the irrational, are accepted. The two truths have indeed something to do with the two "realities," which we might call the "psychological" and the "real" one. Both types share the error of believing that they will find their driving force in the outside world. The introvert is completely extraverted in his thinking, just as the extravert is in his feeling, only the introvert takes possession of the *idea* of the object, whereas the extravert takes possession of the object itself. The introvert thinks with the object, the extravert feels with it. Both are completely rational. But they find their own irrational (i.e., psychological) truth only in themselves, and with it the true source of energy, because life flows from ourselves and not from the object. We are blinded in this respect by the spirit of our age. Not only nations but individuals, too, are alienated from themselves in modernity by interindividual and international relations, and they find the object of their desire always where there is already someone else. This has led to the boundless international superficiality, which is nothing but the mass phenomenon of interindividual normalization and equalization. And the latter phenomenon itself is nothing but the outflow of an archaic *collectivity* that still sticks to people. This collectivity seduces us into the erroneous belief that the other will take the same delight in being used as I do in using him. This naive assumption, which is rooted in collectivity, necessarily leads to mutual fleecing and violating. Although this a priori identity with the object results in an increased adaptation to outer reality, even to the point that we can speak of a worldwide "cultural thought," there is no real advantage in this, neither for a nation nor for the individual, because they both get equalized and lose their intrinsic values. The leveling-out of all external opposites produces big newspapers, excellent railway timetables, fast connections by steamship, international industrial and commercial organizations, and a division of labor that is carried to the extreme. But all of this makes man, who is not a machine but many-sided, sick. *The opposites should be evened out in the individual himself.* True, this will not lead to a general "standard," to a universal ideal of the arts or the sciences, or of production of all kinds; what will emerge is what is generally not accepted but individually valuable, what is internationally regarded as quaint or funny but is nationally valued and alive. For man is not only a herd animal obeying a universal rule but also a "strange" being. It is not only the rational truth of the herd that is vital to him but above all his irrational strangeness, the vital value of which is denied by any outsider, but which is perfectly and immediately evident to the individual; after all, this is what is his very own and his inner vitality! It is not the sameness of nations and individuals, but their extreme diversity and singularity, which is valuable and beautiful in them. With the spirit of international modernity, which is rooted in precisely those vestiges of archaic collectivity, we shall experience the building of a second tower of Babel, which as we know ends in a confusion of tongues. In this way nature helps herself, so that everybody will arrive at what is his own, and though it may, or should, be incomprehensible to the other, it still has the greatest vital value. This is the irrational truth.

I see adaptation to reality in the same way as Fr. Th. [Friedrich Theodor] Vischer views morality, that is, that it is always a matter of self-evidence. Since this adaptation is an endless problem, not constrained by any one side—for "reality" can be expanded interminably—we need some sort of standard, and this standard can be provided only by the subject, never by the object. Although the object can constrain us outwardly, it cannot do the thinking process, which sets norms and limits, for us. The moral law lies within ourselves, not in the object. I have to protect the object against too much experimenting. Even the Freudian way of analysis aims at a change in the subjective attitude, which is brought about by a subjective, psychological process, and not at predominantly experiencing the object and doing something with it.

Experiencing much with the help of the object, however, is tantamount to bringing infantile fantasies into what is concrete. But infantile fantasy is not suited for this, for when it is transferred into the object it becomes the most worthless and objectionable thing, while when being kept within the subject it becomes what is most valuable, namely, the source of anything new and of further development.

The striving for the creation of impersonal values deprives the introvert of a considerable sum of energy in the development of his personality, so that he, just as much as the extravert, in a certain sense falls behind himself (though in the opposite way than the extravert). We must never forget that both types always contain both mechanisms, so that they would be identical, so to speak, if not for the fact that they are completely opposed.

What is certain is that the extravert's abstract feeling does not really love the object, but merely *desires* it. You prove this yourself by your statement that for the extravert the object is *indispensable for his feeling*. Calves and pigs are indispensable for satisfying our hunger, but they would challenge that we love them, for they probably feel quite roughly treated when we lovingly prepare them for a meal. Because of his deficient sensation the extravert believes that his object is naturally delighted by getting his "love," just as he himself is gratified by achieving the fulfillment of his wish. The *feeling* of the extravert *corresponds to outer reality*; calves and pigs are really there to be eaten. The one uses the other, the one devours the other, by cunning and force everybody fights for his place in the sun. And if he does not do it consciously, he does it unconsciously, and then claims that this is love, and he can claim this so long as he senses and feels deficiently. His object, however, does not feel loved at all. The teacher completely ruins the situation for herself, because she senses nothing and thinks nothing, but merely "loves," and because the students are *indispensable for her feeling*. Even though she may have correctly recognized the spirit of outer reality, and of the struggle for life, in her feeling, she still does not recognize the powers of the interior, the power, that is, of her students' sensation and thinking. The students are not cattle for slaughter but human beings who are also struggling for their place in the sun. So I'm saying: precisely because the feeling of the extravert does not correspond to his own inner world (where there is sensation and thinking) but to outer reality with its merciless struggle for life, it is unconsciously completely steeped in the spirit of usurpation and violation. The abstract thinking of the introvert is a parallel to this. It is so much in accordance with outer reality that unconsciously it is completely saturated with, and contingent upon, the lusting for power in the world. We only have to remind ourselves of how pretentious certain philosophical systems act! Naturally the introvert tries to keep his feeling away from his thinking, but this is exactly why, eventually, it will nonetheless find its way into his thinking, in the form of lust for power, where it will occasionally break through with overwhelming force, as in Zarathustra, for example.

It is not feeling and representation that lead to inner reality in the extravert, but only thinking and sensation. Vice versa, for the introvert thinking and sensation lead to the outer world, while feeling and representation lead to inner reality.

It is altogether characteristic of the extravert that he never experiences the conflict in question as irreconcilable, or even tragic, for the simple reason that he does not think, and sense, the object sufficiently enough. He forces the object to fight against that "love" as violently as this "love" is violent itself, because unconsciously he tyrannically takes possession of the object and can neither sense nor think how the object inwardly resists this. A strong and healthy man, who can put up with tastelessness and brutality, and who would rather kill the other than let himself be killed, will enter into this fight to the advantage of both sides. A sensitive and aesthetic man, who cannot put up with brutality, will not enter into this fight, to his and his partner's detriment. And that is tragic. That is why I speak of the possibility of a tragic misunderstanding. On the other hand, we must admire how well nature has arranged this, too. The extravert forces the introvert, through the blindness of his love, to summon in self-defense all the violence and brutality from the depths of his soul, which he so desperately needs in his struggle for life. The energetic resistance of the introvert forces the extravert, in turn, to realize all the shortcomings of his thinking and sensation, which had hampered him in the fight for adaptation in that they prevented him from intellectually grasping the situation adequately.

The introvert has a reactive type of loving but an active type of thinking. The extravert has a reactive type of thinking but an active type of loving. A person's energy is always revealed by his activity. That is his light; his shadow lies in his reactions. So according to the tenor of your last letter, the goal toward which we are moving would promise nothing less than that the shadow will turn into light. With regard to physics, however, we also have to consider our energy balance and its requirements. Is human energy really strong enough, besides maintaining the light it has already created, to turn the shadow into light? I fear we might be on the road to godlikeness, or at least about to create that completely spherical Platonic primordial being, whom, as we know, a god found it necessary to divide into two. If we continue to pursue this road, namely, of compensating ourselves by our own unconscious opposite, we will arrive at fatal mythological analogies, one of which I have already mentioned. For if we succeeded in activating even our shadow, and thereby bring about an all-sided or two-sided activity in ourselves, the shadow of the god would threaten to cut us in two, as it did with Plato's orbicular and perfectly equipped primordial being. As you know, this Platonic myth is a later echo of the earlier, widespread original idea of the first pair of parents, who were pressed together, like a single being, for eons, all-round and positive, until one day a son arose between them, who, to their surprise, separated them. Just as light and shadow always follow one another, positive and negative electricity always attract each other. Two positive charges repel each other, however. Thus we, too, might find that our activated, luminous shadow will suddenly separate itself from our actual light, as if it were repelled by an invisible power that interposes itself between the two centers of activity like a new shadow.

Naturally, this possibility arises only if we assume that it is at all possible to activate the shadow as well. Well, why shouldn't it be possible to raise the merely reactive side in our nature to activity? We are bound, however, to our energy balance. The energy we need to activate the shadow must necessarily be withdrawn from somewhere else. And it can be withdrawn only from a place where energy can be found, that is, from thinking for the introvert, and from feeling for the extravert. Through the withdrawal of energy the active qualities are reduced to the level of a certain dullness. We believe we can see something of the sort in certain oriental psychologies of religion, in which it is precisely the recognition of the shadow that led to the harmonization and leveling-out of the psychological opposites. The legend of the life of Buddha bears testimony to this. And what insights in this respect do we not owe to the superior mind of Lao Tzu!

Jung's Obituary of Hans Schmid-Guisan

Hans Schmid-Guisan: In Memoriam[273]

Life is in truth a battle, in which friends and faithful companions-in-arms sink away, struck by the wayward bullet. Sorrowfully I see the passing of a comrade, who for more than twenty years shared with me the experiment of life and the adventure of the modern spirit.

I first met Hans Schmid-Guisan at a conference of psychiatrists in Lausanne, where I discussed for the first time the impersonal, collective nature of psychic symbols. He was then assistant physician at the Mahaim Clinic in Cery. Not long afterward he came to Zurich, in order to study analytical psychology with me. This collaborative effort gradually broadened into a friendly relationship, and the problems of psychological practice frequently brought us together in serious work or round a convivial table. At that time we were especially interested in the question of the relativity of psychological judgments, or, in other words, the influence of temperament on the formation of psychological concepts. As it turned out, he developed instinctively an attitude type which was the direct opposite of my own. This difference led to a long and lively correspondence, thanks to which I was able to clear up a number of fundamental questions. The results are set forth in my book on types.

I remember a highly enjoyable bicycle tour which took us to Ravenna, where we rode along the sand through the waves of the sea. This tour was a continual discussion which lasted from coffee in the morning, all through the dust of the Lom-

[273]First published in the *Basler Nachrichten*, 25 April 1932. Reprinted here in the translation as published in the *Collected Works*, vol. 18, pp. 760–61.

bardy roads, to the round-bellied bottle of Chianti in the evening, and continued even in our dreams. He stood the test of this journey: he was a good companion and always remained so. He battled valiantly with the hydra of psychotherapy and did his best to inculcate into his patients the same humanity for which he strove as an ideal. He never actually made a name for himself in the scientific world, but shortly before his death he had the pleasure of finding a publisher for his book *Tag und Nacht,* in which he set down many of his experiences in a form peculiarly his own. Faithful to his convictions, he wrote it as he felt he had to write it, pandering to nobody's prejudices. His humanity and his sensitive psychological understanding were not gifts that dropped down from heaven but the fruit of unending work on his own soul. Not only relatives and friends stand mourning today by his bier, but countless people for whom he opened the treasure-house of the psyche. They know what this means to them in a time of spiritual drought.

Bibliography

Note: Jung's works are cited, whenever possible, according to the edition in the *Collected Works* [= CW] (Princeton: Princeton University Press, 1957–83). In order to trace the development of Jung's thoughts, however, in quite a number of cases it has been necessary to quote from the original German publications, not to be found in the CW and the *Gesammelte Werke* [= GW] (Zurich: Rascher; Olten: Walter, 1958–81), in which only later, revised editions were reprinted. Translations of these quotes are our own. Freud's works are cited in the translation of James Strachey et al. in the *Standard Edition of the Complete Psychological Works of Sigmund Freud* [= SE] (London: Hogarth Press, 1956–74).

Adler, Alfred (1912). *Über den nervösen Charakter. Grundzüge einer vergleichenden Individual-Psychologie und Psychotherapie*. Frankfurt am Main: Fischer, 1972. *The Neurotic Character: Fundamentals of a Comparative Individual Psychology and Psychotherapy*. San Francisco: Classical Adlerian Translation Project—Alfred Adler Institute of San Francisco, 2002.

Anonymous (1340). *The Little Flowers of Saint Francis of Assisi*. London: Kegan Paul, Trench Trüber, 1905.

Apuleius, Lucius (2nd half of 2nd century AD). *Metamorphoses, or The Golden Ass*. Trans. William Adlington. Ware, GB: Wordsworth Classics of World Literature, 1996.

Bair, Deirdre (2003). *Jung: A Biography*. New York: Back Bay Books, Little, Brown.

Bancroft, Wilder (1910). New books. [Review of Wilhelm Ostwald, *Große Männer*. Leipzig: Akademische Verlagsgesellschaft, 1909.] *Journal of Physical Chemistry*, 14(1): 88–96.

Bennet, E[dward] A[rmstrong] (1961). *C. G. Jung*. Wilmette, IL: Chiron Publications, 2006.

Bergson, Henri (1907). *Creative Evolution*. Trans. Arthur Mitchell. New York: Henry Holt, 1911. Reprint using original plates: Mineola, NY: Dover Publications, 1998. Online edition of the 1911 translation at http://www.brocku.ca/MeadProject/Bergson/Bergson_1911a/Bergson_1911_toc.html (17 March 2011).

Berquist, Duane H. (n.d.). Paper on Plato's *Meno*. Online at http://www.aristotle-aquinas.org/the-school-of-plato-the-academ/01-dialogues-on-logic/ (5 January 2011).

Binet, Alfred (1903). *L'Étude expérimentale de l'intelligence*. Paris: Schleicher Frères et Cie.

Bleuler, Eugen (1908). Die Prognose der Dementia praecox (Schizophreniegruppe). *Allgemeine Zeitschrift für Psychiatrie*, no. 65: 436–64.

——— (1911). *Dementia praecox oder Gruppe der Schizophrenien*. Vienna: Franz Deuticke.

Brachfeld, Oliver (1954). Gelenkte Tagträume als Hilfsmittel der Psychotherapie. *Zeitschrift für Psychotherapie*, 4: 79–93.

Burkhardt, Carl August Hugo (ed.) (1870). *Goethe's Unterredungen mit dem Kanzler Friedrich von Müller.* Stuttgart: Verlag der J. G. Cotta'schen Buchhandlung. Online at http://openlibrary.org/search?q=burkhardt+goethe+m%C3%BCller (13 January 2011).

Burnham, John C. (1983). *Jelliffe: American Psychoanalyst and Physician, and His Correspondence with Sigmund Freud and Jung*. Ed. William McGuire. Chicago: University of Chicago Press.

Covington, Coline, & Barbara Wharton (eds.) (2003). *Sabina Spielrein: Forgotten Pioneer of Psychoanalysis*. Hove, England: Brunner-Routledge.

Eckermann, Johann Peter (1835). *Gespräche mit Goethe in den letzten Jahren seines Lebens 1823–1932*. Berlin: Deutsche Buch-Gemeinschaft.

Edinger, Edward F. (1985). *Anatomy of the Psyche: Alchemical Symbolism in Psychotherapy*. La Salle, IL: Open Court.

Ellenberger, Henri (1970). *The Discovery of the Unconscious*. New York: Basic Books. German edition: *Die Entdeckung des Unbewußten*. Bern: Hans Huber, 1973.

Ferenczi, Sándor (1909). Introjection and transference. In *First Contributions to Psycho-Analysis*. London: Karnac, 1994, 35–93.

——— (1914). Review of C. G. Jung, *Contribution à l'étude des types psychologiques*. In *Bausteine zur Psychoanalyse,* Band 4, 64–66.

Fordham, Michael (1978). *Jungian Psychotherapy: A Study in Analytical Psychology*. New York: John Wiley & Sons.

Freud, Sigmund (1900). *Die Traumdeutung*. GW II/III. *The Interpretation of Dreams*. SE IV, V.

——— (1912a). Zur Dynamik der Übertragung. GW VIII. The dynamics of transference. SE 12.

——— (1912b). Über neurotische Erkrankungstypen. GW VIII. Types of onset of neuroses. SE 12.

——— (1920). *Jenseits des Lustprinzips*. GW XIII. *Beyond the Pleasure Principle*. SE 18.

Freud, Sigmund, & Karl Abraham (2002). *The Complete Correspondence of Sigmund Freud and Karl Abraham, 1907–1925. Completed Edition*. Ed. Ernst Falzeder. Trans. Caroline Schwarzacher. London: Karnac.

Freud, Sigmund, & Ernest Jones (1993). *The Complete Correspondence of Sigmund Freud and Ernest Jones 1908–1939*. Ed. R. Andrew Paskauskas. Cambridge, MA: Harvard University Press.

Freud, Sigmund, & Carl Gustav Jung (1974). *The Freud/Jung Letters: The Correspondence between Sigmund Freud and C. G. Jung*. Ed. William McGuire. Trans. Ralph Manheim and R. F. C. Hull. Cambridge, MA: Harvard University Press.

Goethe, Johann Wolfgang von (1815). Shakespeare und kein Ende! Online at www.zeno.org/Literatur/M/Goethe,+Johann+Wolfgang (18 January 2011).

——— (1823). Bedeutende Fördernis durch ein einziges geistreiches Wort. Online at www.zeno.org/Literatur/M/Goethe,+Johann+Wolfgang (13 January 2011).

——— (1832). *Faust*. Online at www.zeno.org/Literatur/M/Goethe,+Johann+Wolfgang; English translation by James T. Brooks online at www.einam.com/faust/pages/brooks.html (31 March 2012).

Goodman, Russell B. (ed.) (1995). *Pragmatism: A Contemporary Reader*. New York: Routledge.

Guttman, Samuel A., et al. (eds.) (1995). *Konkordanz zu den Gesammelten Werken von Sigmund Freud*. 6 vols. Waterloo, Ont.: North Waterloo Academic Press.

Hale, Nathan G. (ed.) (1971). *James Jackson Putnam and Psychoanalysis*. Cambridge, MA: Harvard University Press.

Hannah, Barbara (1976). *Jung, His Life and His Work: A Biographical Memoir*. Boston: Shambhala, 1991.

Iselin, Hans Konrad (1982). *Zur Entstehung von C. G. Jungs "Psychologischen Typen." Der Briefwechsel zwischen C. G. Jung und Hans Schmid-Guisan im Lichte ihrer Freundschaft*. Aarau: Sauerländer.

Jacobi, Friedrich Heinrich (1811). *Von den göttlichen Dingen und ihrer Offenbarung*. Leipzig: Fleischer.

Jacobi, Max (ed.) (1846). *Briefwechsel zwischen Goethe und F. H. Jacobi*. Leipzig: Weidmann'sche Buchhandlung. Online at http://

books.google.com/books?id=lMCUfQOlrggC&pg=PR3#v=onepage&q&f=false (7 January 2011).

James, William (1907). *Pragmatism: A New Name for Some Old Ways of Thinking*. New York: Longmans, Green. Reprint in *The Works of William James: Pragmatism*, ed. Fredson Bowers and Ignas K. Skrupselis. Cambridge, MA: Harvard University Press, 1975.

Jehle-Wildberger, Marianne (2009). *Adolf Keller 1872–1963: Pionier der ökumenischen Bewegung*. Zurich: Theologischer Verlag.

Jones, Ernest (1953, 1955, 1957). *The Life and Work of Sigmund Freud*. 3 vols. New York: Basic Books.

Jung, Carl Gustav (1902). *Zur Psychologie und Pathologie sogenannter okkulter Phänomene*. CW 1. *On the Psychology and Pathology of So-Called Occult Phenomena*. CW 1.

——— (1903). Über Simulation von Geistesstörung. GW 1. On simulated insanity. CW 1.

——— (1910). Über Konflikte der kindlichen Seele. *Jahrbuch für psychoanalytische und psychopathologische Forschungen*, 2(1): 33–58. GW 17. Psychic conflicts in a child. CW 17.

——— (1911/12). Wandlungen und Symbole der Libido. *Jahrbuch für psychoanalytische und psychopathologische Forschungen*, 3(1), 1911: 120–227; 4(1), 1912: 162–464. In book form: Leipzig: Deuticke, 1912. Reprint: Munich: Deutscher Taschenbuch Verlag, 1991. In revised form and under new title, *Symbole der Wandlung*, in GW 5; *Symbols of Transformation*, in CW 5.

——— (1912). Neue Bahnen der Psychologie. GW 7. New paths in psychology. CW 7.

——— (1913a). Zur Frage der psychologischen Typen. Vortrag, gehalten am Psychoanalytischen Kongreß in München, September 1913. GW 6. Contribution à l'étude des types psychologiques. *Archives de Psychologie*, 13(52), December 1913: 289–99. A contribution to the study of psychological types. CW 6.

——— (1913b[1912]). Versuch einer Darstellung der psychoanalytischen Theorie. GW 4. The theory of psychoanalysis. CW 4.

——— (1914a). Der Inhalt der Psychose. Nachtrag: Über das psychologische Verständnis pathologischer Vorgänge. GW 3. On psychological understanding [Supplement to The Content of the Psychoses]. CW 3

——— (1914b). Über die Bedeutung des Unbewußten in der Psychopathologie. GW 3. On the importance of the unconscious in psychopathology. CW 3.

——— (1916a). Die Struktur des Unbewußten. GW 7. The structure of the unconscious. CW 7.

——— (1916b). Vorrede zur ersten Auflage der *Collected Papers on Analytical Psychology*. GW 4. Preface to the first edition of the *Collected Papers on Analytical Psychology*. CW 4.

——— (1917a). *Die Psychologie der unbewussten Prozesse. Ein Überblick über die moderne Theorie und Methode der analytischen Psychologie*. Zurich: Rascher. [Original text not included in GW or CW.]

——— (1917b). *Collected Papers on Analytical Psychology*. Ed. Constance Long. London: Ballière, Tindall & Cox.

——— (1919). Instinkt und Unbewußtes. GW 8. Instinct and the unconscious. CW 8.

——— (1921). *Psychologische Typen*. GW 6. *Psychological Types*. Trans. H. Godwin Baynes, revised by R.F.C. Hull. CW 6. First translation into English: *Psychological Types, or The Psychology of Individuation*. Trans. H. Goodwin Baynes. London: Routledge & Kegan Paul, 1923.

——— (1926). *Analytische Psychologie und Erziehung*. GW 17. *Analytical Psychology and Education: Three Lectures*. CW 17.

——— (1928a). Über die Energetik der Seele. GW 8. On psychic energy. CW 8.

——— (1928b). Psychologische Typologie. GW 6, appendix 3. A psychological theory of types. CW 6.

——— (1930/31). Die Lebenswende. GW 8. The stages of life. CW 8.

——— (1931). Vorwort zu Schmid-Guisan, "Tag und Nacht." GW 18/2. Foreword to Schmid-Guisan: "Tag und Nacht." CW 18/2.

——— (1932). Dr. Hans Schmid-Guisan: In memoriam. GW 18/2. CW 18/2.

——— (1935). Grundsätzliches zur praktischen Psychotherapie. GW 16. Principles of practical psychotherapy. CW 16.

——— (1935/36[1943]). *Psychologie und Alchemie*. GW 12. *Psychology and Alchemy*. CW 12.

——— (1936). Psychologische Typologie. GW 6. Psychological typology. CW 6.

——— (1938[1937]). *Psychologie und Religion. Die Terry Lectures 1937 gehalten an der Yale University*. GW 11. *Psychology and Religion (The Terry Lectures)*. CW 11.

——— (1943[1917, 1926]). *Über die Psychologie des Unbewußten*. GW 7. *On the Psychology of the Unconscious*. CW 7.

——— (1945/46). Zur Phänomenologie des Geistes im Märchen. GW 9/1. The phenomenology of the spirit in fairytales. CW 9/1.

——— (1946/47). Theoretische Überlegungen zum Wesen des Psychischen. GW 8. On the nature of the psyche. CW 8.

——— (1951). Grundfragen der Psychotherapie. GW 16. Fundamental questions of psychotherapy. CW 16.

——— (1955). *Mysterium Coniunctionis*. GW 14. CW 14.

——— (1957). *Gegenwart und Zukunft*. GW 10. *The Undiscovered Self (Present and Future)*. CW 10.

——— (1962). *Memories, Dreams, Reflections*. Recorded and edited by Aniela Jaffé. London: Fontana Press, 1995.

——— (1972a). *Briefe I, 1906–1945*. Edited by Aniela Jaffé in collaboration with Gerhard Adler. Olten: Walter.

——— (1972b). *Briefe II, 1946–1955*. Edited by Aniela Jaffé in collaboration with Gerhard Adler. Olten: Walter.

——— (1973a). *Briefe III, 1956–1961*. Edited by Aniela Jaffé in collaboration with Gerhard Adler. Olten: Walter.

——— (1973b). *Letters, Volume 1, 1906–1950*. Selected and edited by Gerhard Adler in collaboration with Aniela Jaffé. London: Routledge & Kegan Paul.

——— (1974). *Letters, Volume 2, 1951–1961*. Selected and edited by Gerhard Adler in collaboration with Aniela Jaffé. London: Routledge & Kegan Paul.

——— (1988). *Nietzsche's Zarathustra. Notes of the Seminar Given in 1934–1939*. Ed. James L. Jarrett. 2 vols. Bollingen Series XCIX. Princeton, NJ: Princeton University Press.

——— (2009). *The Red Book. Liber Novus*. Ed. Sonu Shamdasani. Trans. Mark Kyburz, John Peck, and Sonu Shamdasani. New York: W. W. Norton.

——— (2012). *Introduction to Jungian Psychology: Notes of the Seminar on Analytical Psychology Given in 1925*. Rev. ed. Sonu Shamdasani. Princeton, NJ: Princeton University Press (Philemon Series).

Jung, Carl Gustav, & Franz Riklin (1904/5). Experimentelle Untersuchungen über Assoziationen Gesunder. In *Diagnostische Assoziationsstudien*, vol. 1, 7–145. GW 2. Associations of normal subjects. Trans. Leopold Stein, in collaboration with Diana Riviere. CW 2.

Kerr, John (1993). *A Most Dangerous Method: The Story of Jung, Freud, and Sabina Spielrein*. New York: Alfred A. Knopf.

Korrespondenzblatt (1913). "Ortsgruppe [Branch society] Zürich. Diskussion über Dr. Jungs Libidotheorie" [Discussion on Jung's libido theory]. In *Internationale Zeitschrift für ärztliche Psychoanalyse*, 1: 621–22.

Lao-Tzu (2009). *Taoteching*. Trans. Red Pine. Port Townsend, WA: Copper Canyon Books.

Laozi (2001). *Dao de Jing: The Book of the Way*. Trans. Moss Roberts. Berkeley: University of California Press.

Laplanche, Jean, & Jean-Bertrand Pontalis (1967). *The Language of Psycho-Analysis*. New York: W. W. Norton, 1973.

Maeder, Alphonse (1913). Über das Traumproblem. *Jahrbuch für psychoanalytische und psychopathologische Forschungen*, 5(2): 647–86. *The Dream Problem*. Trans. Frank Mead Hallock and Smith Ely Jelliffe. New York: Nervous and Mental Disease Publishing Company, 1916.

McGuire, William, & R. F. C. Hull (eds.) (1977). *C. G. Jung Speaking: Interviews and Encounters*. Bollingen Series XCVII. Princeton, NJ: Princeton University Press.

Moltzer, Maria (1916a). The conception of the libido and its psychic manifestations. In Shamdasani (1998b), pp. 107–10.

——— (1916b). On the conception of the unconscious. In Shamdasani (1998b), pp. 111–19.

Nietzsche, Friedrich (1885). *Thus Spoke Zarathustra*. Trans. R. J. Hollingsworth. Harmondsworth: Penguin, 1961.

Ostwald, Wilhelm (1909). *Große Männer. Studien zur Biologie des Genies, Bd. 1*. Leipzig: Akademische Verlagsgesellschaft.

Plato (ca. 380–360 BCE). *Phaedo*. In Plato (1961), pp. 40–98.

——— (ca. 385–380 BCE). *Symposium*. In Plato (1961), pp. 526–74. Online at http://classics.mit.edu/Plato/symposium.html (15 March 2011).

——— (1961). *The Collected Dialogues*. Ed. Edith Hamilton and Huntington Cairns. Bollingen Series LXXI. Princeton, NJ: Princeton University Press.

Protokolle des Psychoanalytischen Vereins (Verein für analytische Psychologie), I, January 1913–December 1916. Archives Sonu Shamdasani.

Schiller, Ferdinand Canning Scott (2008). *On Pragmatism and Humanism: Selected Writings, 1891–1939*. Ed. John R. Shook and Hugh P. McDonald. Amherst, NY: Humanity Books.

Schilller, Friedrich von, & Johann Wolfgang von Goethe (1905). *Briefwechsel*. Jena: Diederichs.

Schmid-Guisan, Hans (1931). *Tag und Nacht*. Zurich: Rhein-Verlag.

Shamdasani, Sonu (1998a). *Cult Fictions. C. G. Jung and the Founding of Analytical Psychology*. London: Routledge.

——— (1998b). The Lost Contributions of Maria Moltzer: Two Unknown Papers. *Spring: A Journal of Archetype and Culture*, 64 (*Histories*): 103–19.

——— (2003). *Jung and the Making of Modern Psychology: The Dream of a Science*. Cambridge: Cambridge University Press.

——— (2005). *Jung Stripped Bare by His Biographers, Even*. London: Karnac.

——— (2009). Introduction. In Jung (2009).

Shapiro, Kenneth Joel, & Irving E. Alexander (1975). *The Experience of Introversion: An Integration of Phenomenological, Empirical, and Jungian Approaches*. Durham, NC: Duke University Press.

Simmer, Hans H. (1978). Ostwalds Lehre vom Romantiker und Klassiker. Eine Typologie des Wissenschaftlers. *Medizin-historisches Journal*, 13: 277–96.

Smith, Amy C. (2003). Athenian political art from the fifth and fourth centuries BCE: Images of historical individuals. In C. W. Blackwell (ed.), *Dēmos: Classical Athenian Democracy* (A. Mahoney and R. Scaife, eds., *The Stoa: a consortium for electronic publication in the humanities* [www.stoa.org]), edition of 18 January 2003. Contact: cwb@stoa.org

Spitteler, Carl (1906). *Imago*. Reprint, Frankfurt am Main: Suhrkamp, 1979.

Swann, Wendy (ed.) (2011). *Memoir of Tina Keller-Jenny. A Lifelong Confrontation with the Psychology of C. G. Jung*. New Orleans, LA: Spring Journal.

Taylor, Eugene (1980). Jung and William James. *Spring: A Journal of Archetype and Culture*, 20: 157–69.

van der Post, Laurens (1976). *Jung and the Story of Our Time*. Harmondsworth: Penguin, 1985.

Waley, Arthur (1958). *The Way and Its Power: A Study of the Tao Te Ching and Its Place in Chinese Thought*. New York: Grove Press.

Wittenberger, Gerhard, & Christfried Tögel (eds.) (2001). *Die Rundbriefe des "Geheimen Komitees."* Band 2: *1921*. Tübingen: edition diskord.

Wolfensberger, Giorgio J. (ed.) (1995). *Suzanne Perrottet, ein bewegtes Leben. Text und Bilder*. Weinheim, Berlin: Beltz Quadriga.

Index